NEVER WALK
When You Can Ride

NEVER WALK
When You Can Ride

by **MIKE McFARLAND**
Illustrated by **JOE BEELER**

NORTHLAND PUBLISHING

Contents

An Apology
and Dedication

First off, I want to make an apology to any scholars that might pick up this book. I ain't no author and don't want to be responsible for any heart failure to any grammar critics. If you are sensitive to improper English, I suggest that you stop right here. It's like the cowpuncher who asked the other ol' boy to stay for supper. He hollered "chuck," then added, "but if you don't like frijoles, supper's over!"

I happened on this project by accident. When I was not much more than a kid, I went to work for the Greene Cattle Company (O R O). Whistle Mills was the wagon boss and always kept a diary. Just before Whistle died he was kind enough to give me his diaries from the past twenty years—a gift I will always treasure.

I knew it was mainly used for a permanent tally book, but every so often he would make a comment that tipped his hand that he had written down anything exciting or unusual that happened. I liked the idea, and bein' I have a damn poor memory, I started scribbling down some of the stories I heard and some of the things I saw. I have kept a diary from that time on, sometimes faithfully and at other times not so faithfully. I didn't have no idea about writin' a book at that time. It just struck me that some of the stories I was hearing might never be told again and some of the ol' boys that were tellin' 'em wouldn't be ridin' this range much longer. So I want to put in my personal thanks to Whistle for gettin' me started.

The West has gotten to be a popular subject the last few years. Artists and authors have jumped in with both feet to reap the profits. I don't blame 'em for wantin' to cash in when the chips are stacked so high, but, with a few exceptions, most of these fellers don't know what they're writin' or paintin' about. These fellers write and paint *about* cowboys — something they don't savvy.

I just want to set the ledger straight. The stories in this book are all true — true by cowboy standards. Cowpunchers have big imaginations and sometimes the truth has to be stretched for the sake of a story — so like saying, these are all true *cowboy* stories, not true stories *about* cowboys.

I don't claim to be an author. Mr. Webster says an author is the originator or creator of a book. I don't create or originate nothin'. I leave that up to Almighty God. I give Him the credit for creatin' the ranges and the men who work them. I just want to thank Him for lettin' me be a part of his masterpiece, and so I dedicate this book to Him.

Glossary

Auger   To talk or visit

Barlow   Pocket knife

Beeves   Cow brute butchered for food

B.L.M.   Bureau of Land Management; part of the federal government's program to keep unqualified people in work

Bleuchers   Custom, handmade boots made by the Bleucher Boot Company

Britchen   Strap around mule's butt to keep pack from slipping forward

Brown's Mule   Brand of chewing tobacco

Bull Durham   Brand of smoking tobacco used for "rolling your own"

Burg   Town

Button   A young kid

Caballo   Mexican word for horse

Camp   House located apart from the main ranch headquarters to allow a cowboy to take care of the surrounding country

Cavey   Northern term that refers to an outfit's saddle horses; remuda in the Southwest

Cayuse   Horse

Chaps   Leather leggins worn for protection

Chappin'   The act of applying chaps to the backside of another in such a manner as to inflict great pain. Generally done for punishment after conviction in a kangaroo court.

Chili Eater   Slang for a Mexican

Cholla   Very spiney cactus, sometimes called Jumping Cholla

Chuck   Food

Comida   Mexican word for food

Corriente   Cow brute of indescript breeding

Cut   *a* Cut—Cattle separated from a herd and held together for some reason (such as to sell); *to* Cut—The act of separating (cuttin') cattle from a herd

Dally   To take several wraps around the horn of a saddle with a rope after having caught a cow brute; will hold tight till the wraps are taken off

Doggies   Calves with no mothers

Drive   Refers to the method of rounding up cattle by having the cowboys scattered over a large piece of country and driving their cattle to one meeting place called a roundup ground

Flaxey   Blond-colored mane and tail

Frijoles   Mexican word for pinto beans

Gringo   Mexican slang for a U.S. citizen

Gumbo   Thick, sticky mud

Gunsel   An individual with no knowledge of livestock

Habla   Mexican word for talk

Hacienda   Mexican word for home

Haired Over   Refers to a country that is covered over with thick brush or trees

Hard-Tail   Mule

Hock   Joint in the hind leg of a cow, horse, or mule

Hold Up   Place where cattle that are being gathered come together and are stopped by cowboys

Hood   Short for hoodlum; the man an outfit hires to help the cook with such things as chopping wood, washing dishes, and peeling spuds

Hoolihan   A loop thrown over the head with the wrist turned backwards; used for catching horses because the rope is not swung before being released, thus not exciting the remuda

Hoss   Horse

Hunker Down   To squat down

Java   Coffee

Jefe   Mexican word for chief or second in command

Jerk   When gathering a rough country, only a small piece of country is worked at a time (versus a flat country where large pieces of country can be worked at one time); one of these small drives is referred to as a jerk

Jigger   Second in command

Leche   Mexican word for milk

Lift, on the   Refers to cows so weak that they require help to get up after lying down

Long Rope   When someone brands another's calves (steals or rustles cattle), he is said to carry a long rope

Malapai   A kind of volcanic rock

McCarty   A lead rope tied to a hackamore or snaffle bit

Morale   A feed bag made of burlap; used to feed horse grain

Outfit   Ranch

Paunch   The large stomach or rumen of a cow brute

Pills   The boss's orders; thus when the boss "spills his pills," this means he has given his orders

Prolapsed Cow   A cow who's vagina has inverted and is protruding due to straining

Prowl   To ride and look at the country and livestock

Rawhide   Untanned hide from a cow brute used for making and braiding hackamores, reins, and reatas

Rawhide Outfit   Denotes a ranch held together by rawhide; a cheap outfit

Reata   Rope made out of braided rawhide

Remuda   Mexican word used in the Southwest that refers to the outfit's saddle horses; cavey in the North

Roundup   (1) A herd of cattle just gathered; (2) Refers to the whole period of time and all the work involved in gathering a ranch's cattle

Running Iron   A branding iron made like a hook or a cinch ring held by two green sticks; in this case the brand is "drawn" on the animal

Rollers in a Horse's Nose   A rattling noise made by a horse when he's spooked

Saddle   Refers to a low place or pass between two higher hills

Savvy   Knowledge

Shelly Cow   Old cow

Sleeper   Calf that has been earmarked but not branded

Smudge   Smoke

S.O.B. Stew   Stew made from the heart, tongue, liver, sweatbreads, and marrowgut

Soogans   Originally, goose-down quilt but may mean blankets in general

Stamp Iron   Branding iron formed in the shape of the finished brand, thus it needs only to be stamped on and not drawn

Stays   Staves of a fence; cowpunchers never say "staves"

Tamaters   Tomatoes

Tie Hard   To tie the end of a rope solid to the saddle horn

U.S.F.S.   United States Forest Service; a part of the federal government, Department of Agriculture, trained in the art of harassing the cowman

Waddie   Cowboy

Wagon   General term referring to all the men, equipment, and work involved in a roundup on an outfit large enough that it requires the crew to move from place to place always camping close to their work

Water Gap   The part of a fence that crosses a wash or canyon and is subject to being washed out by high water

Woolies   Wild and wooly cowboys

Works   Common term for roundup

Work a Herd   To cut or separate a herd

Yearling   One-year-old

COW
CAMP
BEEF

The R O Sharpshooters

Ol' Brushy claims that butcherin' is one of the most common-place events and, yet, one of the most unpredictable that takes place on a cow outfit. Seein' that I don't quite foller this line, he takes a chew, settles down (ol' Brushy claims that you should never walk when you can ride and never stand when you can sit), then tells this piece of history to prove he knows what he says.

"It's been some years back but not so distant that it would be best to sleeper the cowboys in this story, 'cause they're both good hands and both still in the country. The outfit is in northern Arizona and runs the O R O brand. One ol' boy has been workin' for this Iron for nearly thirty years, and the youngun' has been there for nearly thirty days.

"The new one's anxious to show that he's no slouch and allows how he's something to behold with a rifle. So when they get some beeves penned, the ol' timer hands the rifle to the button.

"Now, maybe this kid's a shot and maybe he ain't. Maybe the old man breathin' down the kid's neck and trying to look through the sights at the same time he does has got the kid nervous, or maybe the heifer moved just as he squeezed her off. Anyway, the ball hits low and just draws blood on the heifer's nose. The only thing that hits the ground is that youngster's pride!

"It don't excite the old man, but the boy gets a mite hasty, and the first bloody head that sticks out of that milling bunch also gets a ball in the nose!

"This time, the ol' man figures it's time to put some experience behind the sights. He don't realize it but his blood pressure is up a bit and he's trying to figure how he's going to explain two beeves hanging from the gate crossbars when another bloody head peeks out and he lets her have it. Well, she goes down, but while he's cutting her throat to let her bleed, the kid is making an inspection and drawls out in his calmest voice, 'I believe you got another one, 'cause I don't see where I hit this one!' I'm afraid that little statement didn't do much to improve those two's relationship, and with the oaths the old man is cutting loose with, that air's so thick that a buzzard would bog down in midflight!

"By the time those two bowlegged sharpshooters get finished, there's three beeves hanging up at Oaks and Willows that night and they finish by the moon!

"It's a good thing that the spring branding wagon is about to pull out and they're putting on extra help, 'cause the nights are warm and they don't have any coolers to hang the meat in back then."

Ol' Brushy says, "The kid tells me years later that he felt obligated to eat as much beef as he could—and he dang near foundered hisself trying to eat it up before it spoils!"

Showdown at
Pica Camp

By readin' the newspaper and listenin' to some of these fellers comin' home from that Vietnam War, I gather that the army has taken to the idear that sharpshooters don't win wars. They claim that it's the amount of lead a man can scatter that counts. With these new rifles they're packing, they can durn sure put out a lot of lead and in a hurry. But if you remember right, you could hardly say we won that war!

Ol' Brushy swears that a little sharpshootin' might have helped the stars and stripes in that tussle. Takin' a chew of tobacca, he starts in like this, "Now, I never seen any action across the big pond when I was in the army, so I suppose some of you might argue with what I got to say; but before you get fighty, hear me out and I'll tell you what makes me think it's so.

"It all takes place at Pica Camp, just twenty miles out of Seligman, Arizona. I'm workin' with the fall wagon at the time, but it just so happens that the wagon is at Pica, and bein' that's where my family is stayin', I give my cowboy bed a rest and camp in the house with my wife and two kids.

"Well, it's getting along late in the evening, and the wagon boss has cut about four fellers off to butcher a beef. I've already went home for the evening when the shootin' starts.

"It don't bother me none when I hears the first three shots 'cause

I've witnessed many a butcherin' that required three shots to bring a beef down, but I gets a mite curious and peeks out the door when I hear the next three shots.

"Now, Pica Camp sits in the middle of a big flat, which is about twenty-seven miles long and as wide as twelve miles at one end. But the way they built that camp, you'd 'a thought it was a mountain outfit and the size of the flat had forced 'em to bunch up the pens, house, and barn.

"The barn rears up off that flat like a misplaced skyscraper and I never figured out whether they built the house in the pens or built the pens around the house. I have given it considerable thought, however, and I believe that the ol' boy that was the architect of that maze of livestock boogers had 'er figured so that the flies would guarantee that no cowpuncher would try to shade up in the house! I'll tell a man, I've seen the sides of that white house turn plumb black with the swarmin' varmints.

"Well, I had no more than stepped to the door when I realize that the wife is peerin' past me, sizen' up the situation and eyeing the kids who are hanging on the fence and watchin', too!

"Jack, the cowpuncher that's doing the shootin', has got a double-action Colt's .22 six-shooter and he's reloading. He's standing in the middle of a big lot about three hundred feet long, and at the far end, in a corner, is a two-year-old Brahmer cross-bred steer.

"After reloadin', he tries to close in on Mr. Steer for a better shot, but the steer don't see it that way and he starts for the other end! The cowboy tries to head him, but bein' he's afoot and with them high-heeled boots he's a wearin' he don't make no more of an impression on Mr. Steer than a lame duck. He's hell for try, though, and when he sees he can't turn the steer, he opens up with ol' smokey. Even after the steer passes, he is still a pullin' that trigger and runnin' for all he is worth!

"This runnin' has changed the line of fire some, and although we aren't in immediate danger, the little lady comes by me runnin' wide open and went around those kids fast enough to do justice to any waddie that ever led a drive in wide open country and gathering runnin' cattle. She was around 'em, had 'em turned, and penned in the house before Jack had his third shot fired, and he was jerkin' on that trigger like he was scratchin' gnat bites!

"By this time, the whole crew had been drawn by all the shootin'

and there was quite an audience gathered.

"The cowpuncher is reloadin' again and the steer has retreated back to his corner. The way Jack is a puffin' and the way that steer is eyen' Jack, I'm beginning to wonder if that Diamond A wagon is going to have beef or cowpuncher on the rail by nightfall. If Jack don't improve his performance any, I'm bettin' on the steer.

"Well, the waddie closes in again; this time ol' steer makes a run at him but turns off at the last second. If Jack had took a step forward and hit that steer over the head with that pea-shooter instead of runnin' backwards and a shootin', he'd 'a come closer to getting the steer down!

"The steer goes around the lot in the opposite direction this time and Jack never lets up. The cowpunchers that were watchin' ain't to be seen and they don't raise their heads 'til they count all six shots!

"My wife has thrown both kids to the floor and she's layin' over the top of 'em like an old mother hen.

"When the boss raises up, he's runnin' for his pickup. He comes back unholsterin' a service model automatic Colt .45. I notice several cowpunchers slippin' sly grins at each other and I warn my wife not to let the kids up.

"By this time the boss has got everybody's attention, includin' Jack's, and the spotlight's on him. He seems to sense the fact and I'll tell ya that John Wayne would'a been a might jealous the way that gentleman swaggered into that pen!

"Mindin' his rangeland manners, Jack steps back and lets the wagon boss have his chance. When the steer breaks, the boss is shootin' and runnin' at the same time, but when Mr. Steer don't go down, it's too much for Jack and he opens up, too!

"There's a lot of lead flyin': one man with a double action six-shooter and the other with an automatic pistol! I'll bet them army generals would have been real proud of these two rapid-fire artists! You'd'a swore a heel-fly couldn't have flown through that wall of lead but Mr. Steer just picks up speed. As the steer rounds the lot and I dive back in the door, I'm thinkin' this is about as close to warfare as I've ever been!

"Jack's done shot up a box of twenty-two shells, and the wagon boss has went through three clips of cartridges, and about the only thing they have accomplished is to skin up the ol' steer when he runs into the fence — and that don't seem to slow him none.

"Jack finally quits when he trips over his tongue that he's been draggin' for the last three laps.

"When the boss sees it's a one-man show, he goes to hollerin' for someone to bring him his 30-30. A cowpuncher takes him his rifle out of fear that this madman might still have one more shell in his pistol.

"The boss finally downs the steer, cowpunchers start comin' out from behind cover, and I allow as how my wife can let the kids up.

"Next morning one of the cowboys allows the steer died of heart failure 'cause they never did find a hole that could have stopped him. He claims, 'Most of the damage comes from runnin' into fences, and he must have lost a lot of blood that way, 'cause when we cut his juglar, we couldn't have filled a shot glass with the blood we get!'

"Later on, one ol' boy who's worked for the outfit for nineteen years claims he wouldn't be wearin' store-bought teeth now if it wasn't for all the lead he's chewed on all these years!

"Yes sir, I'll bet the army would like to buy into that outfit, just for a training ground!"

Vermejo
Park Beef

▼▼▼▼▼▼▼

There's a sure enough art in selecting a beef on a cow outfit. Seems like everyone has got a different idear as to what makes good eatin'! The common waddie wants to eat the best critter in the herd, and the boss wants to eat the sorriest critter in the herd, or that's how it seems from each other's point of view. 'Course the cowboy's view is strickly from one who has to eat the beef; the boss's view is strictly based on economics.

I found the best way to get a beef is to send one man; otherwise, you're sure to end up with a couple'a men arguin' about the finer points of beef judgin'.

Coley Lyons tells a story that takes place on the big Vermejo Park Ranch many years ago. He had just left Texas and was with the Vermejo Park wagon. He said, "It was a big crew, lots of good cowboys and it was the kind of country where they throwed together some purty big herds.

"The management sent word out to the wagon that they needed to see the wagon boss, so puttin' his jigger in charge, he pulls out for headquarters. He knows the cook is about out of beef, so before he leaves he tells the jigger, 'You need to butcher tonight.' Then as a second thought, he throws in, 'Find somethin' that don't fit the bunch.'

"The wagon boss knows he's got a good jigger and always

figured he was mighty clever, but never knew how clever until he gets back to the wagon a couple of days later. Ridin' up to the wagon, he sees hanging on a fence the hide from the new beef. He recognized it right off and lays for his jigger when he comes in. He gets his chance after the cook hollers chuck and someone 'lows at how the new beef is sure tender! The wagon boss comments, 'It oughta be, it was the best heifer in the herd!' It don't take the jigger long to counter, 'You told us to butcher somethin' that didn't fit the bunch. Well, that's what we did — all the rest are corriente sons'a bitches!"

RANGE WOMEN

Wagon
Widders

▰▰▰▰▰▰

These modern times has brought a lot of luxury to this ol' world. It's hard to find a home without every kind of new gadget you can imagin'. They got everything from electric can openers to ovens that can sizzle a turkey in less time than it takes to run ol' Tom down and chop his head off! There's few homes that ain't got two cars parked in front of it and a boat behind it and with all these labor savin' devices these women got, it's a cinch the tires on their cars hardly got time to cool off before they jump in 'em again and go to the next bridge club meetin'!

Things are different for ranch women, always have been and always will be. Family life has always been tough on ranches. There never was many cow camps fit enough to ask a woman to live in. Most camps was originally built for a couple of bachelors and ain't had a new nail drove in 'em since the last peg was driven fifty to sixty years ago. They was built close to the middle of the country a man was supposed to look after, and of course, this put these camps a long ways from any kind of schoolin' for the little ones. Most roads originated as two-track wagon roads or pack trails, dependin' on how rough the country is, and many of these roads ain't seen a blade over the top of 'em yet!

For such reasons, there's been many a cowpuncher who's had to board his family in town while he did the only work he loved and knew.

Coley Lyons says this talk brings to mind a story of an ol' 3 V cowpuncher he works with one time. The ol' 3 V outfit sat where the Diamond A outfit in northern Arizona is located today but it took in a lot more country back then, and seein' that the Diamond A country takes in just under a million acres now, that 3 V outfit was sure enough a big piece of country. There wasn't many fences back then, and the wagons they run to do the gatherin' and brandin' stayed out nearly year-round, barrin' a few months in the winter and a short spell in the summer.

It's one of these wagon cowboys that I hear the story about. He's got his family camped at Seligman, a little railroad town on the south end of the ranch.

Even though he takes advantage of every chance to go see his family, it's long spells between trips to town, and every time he goes, it seems his kids has grown a foot since he's seen 'em last. It's on one of these vists he learns he's a stranger in his own home.

Without thinking, he stops and knocks at the door. One of his towheaded kids answers the door, and upon seein' his dad standin' there, runs back through the house a hollerin' "Mommy! Mommy! That cowboy is here again!"

Yes sir, there has been many a lonely family waitin' for the wagon to pull in, whether they was in town or stuck out in some cow camp.

Times have changed a few of these camps to where they are nicer to live in, but it hasn't changed the distance to schools and many lonely days that turn into weeks, and weeks into months on these big outfits that still run a wagon. I guess it's a long span of time between visits home for these cowboys that has labeled their wives "wagon widows." Like all he-folks, some cowboys treat their wives better'n others. As a rule, most keep the wood box and the lanterns full of fuel for the "little lady" when they are camped at home. As I've said before, though, there's long spells between bein' "camped at home," and "bein' with the wagon," resultin' in some pretty calloused hands that used to be soft and pretty before she got charmed by this "bold knight of the saddle" with all his stories of the romance of the West!

Like I said, some takes good care of their women and some don't; but as a rule, they savvy the hardship their she-folks go through and do their best to ease the agony of it all. But, even the best of 'em slip once in a while, and it ain't long till this tender thing in lace and calico figures out a way to change this rough ol' cowdog into a hand-lickin' pup once again!

Ol' Brushy knows of such a woman and tells it this way. "There's a small crew, maybe five men, working out of Francis Creek some years back. Rusty Criner's the camp man then and his wife is there with him. This crew ain't going to be there long and the boss asks Mrs. Criner if she'd do the cookin' for them.

"Things go good for two days. Then Rusty forgets to check the wood box one evenin' and as they're leavin' camp the next mornin' his wife hollers, 'Rusty! There's no wood chopped!' At which Rusty throws back over his shoulder, 'We ain't takin' the axe!' Now, Rusty really hee-hawed over that and enjoyed hisself all day a thinkin' back on it. It was a long day and he had a lot of time to smile to hisself; but his smile faded away when they jogged back into camp.

"They was so hungry they'd been chewin' on sticks for the last five miles a tryin' to ease the pain in their gut. The sun was out of sight when they turns their ponies loose and start for the house.

"Rusty's wife is there in the kitchen, busy as ever and has got 'er all ready for the boys when they walk through the door. And there, a sittin' on the table, is the saddest sight them punchers ever seen.

"There's a platter of raw steaks, a pot of frijoles that rattles, a bowl full of raw spuds, and a gob of raw bisquit dough in a pan! The coffee pot's full but the grounds are still floatin' and it's a cinch it ain't got no hotter than that room all day!

"Them boys stops in their tracks and it's so quiet that a fly sounds like a buzz saw as he rounds the kitchen and sets down on the cold stove. Them that's brave enough, sneak a look at Mrs. Criner, who's standin' there with her hands on her hips. Right about then she's as friendly as a diamondback and sore as a boil. Them boys go to slippin' through that door like they was just about to witness a murder and afraid it would be theirs! Rusty's the first one out and it's a race to the woodpile. You never seen cowboys so fast with an axe! The chips sure flew and it wasn't no time till the smoke was a curlin' from the stove pipe.

"Mrs. Criner was game and seein' she held the ace and the boys had cashed in she cooks a meal them boys are a long time rememberin'.

"Rusty had a full winter's supply of wood piled by the house, and when them boys leave, there ain't a chunk in sight that don't fit that cook stove!"

Bear Creek
Shovel

▰▰▰▰▰

Some years back Cole Moorhouse and his wife was camped at the Bear Creek Camp on the O R O Ranch. This was sure enough a cowboy's camp 'cause there ain't no electricity, no butane stove, or none of the modern contraptions that break down and keep a man afoot rather than ahorseback. The camp sits right in the middle of this country, with just a mile or two of fence in all of it.

The country's turnin' green and there's lots of calves on the ground. It's springtime and Cole thinks he's died and went to Heaven! But there's something that turns sour on Cole. As things turn green, JoAnn starts to thinkin' how nice it'd be to have a garden! If Cole would just get a shovel from headquarters and turn a little sod for her, she'd have fresh tamaters by the middle of August.

It's sometime in the middle of July when we hear how easy JoAnn is and how far Cole will go to keep from usin' a shovel. Cole and JoAnn are into headquarters after groceries and I guess it's the canned tamaters that JoAnn's boxing up to take back to Bear Creek that shakes her memory and she says, "It sure is a shame this outfit don't allow the cowboys to have shovels in their camps. We could have had a real nice garden this summer!"

THE PROUD BREED

The
Proud Breed

▼▼▼▼▼▼

Cowpunchers are a proud breed and many find it just downright insulting to do anything that requires any footwork. Ol' Brushy claims, "Any fool can see that the good Lord made the human foot to fit a stirrup. Why, if he had figured on us to do much walkin' he'd'a built us with hooves!"

Some of these royal-blooded aristrocrats hump and swell up like an ol' pack mule if you'd tell 'em to do somethin' that wasn't ahorseback. It's not that they're lazy, 'cause you could hardly call a man lazy that crawls out of his soogans before light every morning and will work till dark or later in rain or snow, if need be.

No, they ain't lazy, just proud. Somewhere, along through the years, they've come to figure that they're professionals. And I'll allow as how they have got it figured about right! Any man that has ever run a cow outfit will testify to the truth of it.

Ol' Brushy and I were in the Palace Bar in Prescott a sippin' the smart juice they peddle there, when ol' Brushy cuts loose with a cussin' that would turn a blizzard around and send it home with a suntan! He's a cussin' some of these so-called ranch managers that are plaguing the cow country these days.

"They say they can't find no cowboys these days! Well, they'd have cowboys, and good ones, if they worked and ran their ranches like cowmen. I never saw an outfit that was ever short of help, if it was run right. Oh, every once in a while a man will slip up and hire one too many "slick ears" and end up worse off than he was before.

"I wasn't there, but I hear the story told about the Fort Rock Ranch south and west of Seligman," ol' Brushy raves on. "Pete Criner's the boss and sure enough cowboy. Pete don't have much patience with anyone who'd hire out as a cowpuncher then can't back it up. Well, he's got him one of those kind of fellers in one of his camps and it don't take Pete long to figure it out after one pass through this feller's country. Now, Pete ain't very gentle with this so-called cowboy when he visits his camp, but knowin' this man has got a wife and two little ones to feed, he don't tell him to leave. He figures it's just a short while before he can scare this feller off the place and that will give him time to plan for his family.

"It's a busy time of year with waters dryin' up and cows to move. This feller does savvy that much and when he senses that he's no longer welcome, he goes to Pete and says, 'I'm going to leave, Pete. But I sure hate to quit when you're so far behind in your work.'

"A slow grin comes over Pete's face as he shakes the man's hand and says, 'Don't worry ol' Pard, I'll be all caught up as soon as you're gone!'

"But those kind ain't cowboys. I'm talking about the kind that know their work and ain't afraid to do it. I don't know whether it's the long hours in the saddle that affects 'em, the dry days in the sun that bakes their brain, the rain that drowns it, or the snow that freezes it, but whatever, it ain't unlikely that one of these ol' boys thinks it's damned near impossible for him to walk without help of a caballo between his bowed legs.

"I suppose these bowlegs don't fit in with a lot of these new ranch managers. They claim they can't find any decent cowboys but what they really mean to say is when they find somebody that's a dandy fence builder, truck driver, windmill puller, and mechanic and don't mind milking a cow or mowing the boss's lawn or saddlin' his horse for him, he's no good at handlin' livestock! Now, the reason they can't figure it out is 'cause these ol' boys know more about them kind of chores than they do about livestock and cowpunchers. It's more important to them to see the home ranch sparklin' with new white fences, fresh pruned lawns and trees than it is to have some feller out prowlin' amongst his cows. Trouble is, cowpunchers ain't that easily satisfied; cowpunchers sleep best when they know what's going on in their country and they have to be ahorseback to do that!"

Whistle

▼▼▼▼▼▼

By God this is mule country!" squalled Whistle as he dug another shovelful of malapai gumbo out from under the bogged-down Dodge power wagon. "What in the hell are we doing here with a pickup, anyway? This is mule country, I tell ya!"

Every time I get stuck, or even come close to gettin' stuck, Whistle's words come to me as if he was sittin' alongside and scoldin' me for usin' a pickup. Little beads of sweat break out on my face as if he was cussin' me and tellin' me, "I told you so, Button!" Whistle knew the country, if anybody did. He came to northern Arizona when he was nineteen years old. He rode out from Prescott through the Camp Wood country, crossed the Baca Float Number Five Land Grant, and joined a wagon camped at the old E L Ranch on the Muddy. It was a wide open country back then with lots of wild cattle. This suited him to a tee and he stayed in this country most of his life from then on, outside of a few hitches he puts in on the Mohave Desert (he always called it "Moharve"), the Cataract Plains, and one hitch he puts in at Castle Hot Springs. He was always ashamed of the last and there's few people knows he wrangled dudes for a while! He always shrugged it off with, "I was young then and there was plenty of wiskey and women. I'll tell ya one thing, though, it didn't last long, and if it hadn't been for all the added attractions and my age, I wouldn't have tried it at all! Anyway, I wasn't long in findin' out that I was in the wrong place, and bein' I never had the silver tongue it took to woo these maidens, I pulled out and never looked back."

Wild cows and rough country is what suited Whistle and he spent most of his life around just those two things. In later years, nothin' brightened up the man's eyes like the talk of wild cattle. He built quite a reputation as a man that could run to a cow. A puncher once claimed that if a man should have ever wanted to get rid of Whistle, all's he would have had to do was to have the guts to fall in behind Whistle when he was runnin' a cow brute and holler at him, Get out of my way—you're too slow! "Trouble is," he added, "I never seen anyone that could do it!"

Jack George, who became famous in his own right as one of the old time cranky wagon cooks, told me about a time when he was younger and still punchin' cows. It's in the spring of the year, they've made a gather, changed horses, worked the herd, branded the calves, and are leaving with the cut to a holding pasture. The cut is made up mostly of yearlings and just a few ol' shelly cows that were missed the fall before. There ain't a yearlin' in the bunch that likes the setup and they handle about as nice as a covey of quail. It would be hard to handle this bunch if you had plenty of room and plenty of help, but this rough and brushy country makes it hard to always be in the right place at the right time, and it seems like a man ought to be in ten places all at the same time.

When they leave with the cut, Jack says Whistle's in the lead and him and Buck Smith are on point sides of Whistle. Jack says, "The horse I'm riding is the best horse in my mount; he could sure fly to a cow. He had a way of running over brush and rocks that just seemed to smooth 'er out. When a man opened that pony up off the side of a mountain, he just turned it into a boulevard! Anyhow, I'm sure mounted and I'm just waiting for something to come out by me!

"Whistle's mounted on a mule, and I'm startin' to picture how many of these yearlin's I'm gonna tie down before we get to the holdin' pasture. Now, I always respected and liked Whistle but I figured that this time I'm holding the ace and I'm gonna show him how to catch a yearlin'! I didn't have to make a hole, hell no, it was just a matter of time before something split out by us. Them yearlin's was sure goosey and there was one big steer that was lookin' for a way out. He's hot right from the start, got his head up as high as she'll go, and he's steppin' high. He don't walk but trots out in the lead then stops sudden, head jerkin' and shakin', slobberin' and lookin' wild-eyed at everything and not seein' nothin'. His tail's wringin' and his rear end is smeared with green, plumb up on his back. He stays like this till the other yearlin's catch up with him; then instead of stayin' with 'em he jumps out in front again. Everybody's got their rope down, and even though Whistle holds them up a couple of times to let them quiet down, Mr. Steer just gets worse. We finally top a ridge and when we tip off the other side the ball opens. It's more than the steer can stand when he starts downhill and he breaks out between me and Whistle like a runaway freight train. Whistle and I try to plug the hole but can't get there; the best we can do is turn the rest of the yearlin's back. We both stay long enough to see that they are gonna hold up, then we both whirl and leave after the steer. I'm smilin' all over, and bein' the way we both leave at the same time and the steer

is out of sight, it's a race to see who can get there first. I'm still grinnin' when we hit the brush and I lose sight of Whistle. He's off to
my left somewhere when I catch sight of the steer as he goes around
a cedar tree a ways ahead of me. I'm bending over and thinkin' how
this is one steer I'm gonna beat Whistle to, but just then I hear Mr.
Steer bawl and I and I know the race is over!

   "I had Whistle beat every way—had the deck stacked in my
favor—but Whistle had an ace for a hole card, too. He had that
something that only a few men have: that built-in instinct it takes
to get to a wild cow right now. It's not something someone can tell
you how to do, it's just something some men have and others don't.
Whistle had it!"

   Not only could Whistle get to a cow in a hurry, but he could
do something when he got there. He was a sure enough good hand
with a rope. . .and purty, too. Even as an old man in his late seven-
ties he would stand up in his stirrups, and swingin' his rope over his
head (not like lots of men that age who swing a rope down on their
side), he could sure crack it on something.

   Most cowpunchers don't get good at ropin' by accident: it takes
practice, and Whistle wasn't no exception. Once when I was nothing
more than a button, the R O wagon was camped at Mohone. Me
and another kid had a cow skull wired to an old stump and were prac-
ticing roping it. Whistle walked by and dropped the comment, "When
I was your age, I practiced on movin' horns." And I'll bet he did!

   Bein' that Whistle was conscientious and always thinkin' about
what was best for the company and sure enough savvied the wild
cow, it was only natural that it wouldn't be long before he was runnin' the R O wagon. They had plenty of wild cattle back then and
it was a safe bet that he had the savvy to run a crew and catch the
cows that needed catchin' and handle the rest so's they got gentler
as the years went by. He took to the job like a horse takes to corn,
and when he turned the wagon over to Buck Smith in 1972 (Whistle was 76 years old then), the cows handled a whole lot different
for Buck than they did for Whistle. He always gathered by usin' small,
short jerks into a holdup, no big wide-open drives, and you could
purty well bet that when a works was over there was darn few cows
on the outfit that hadn't been in a roundup. There weren't many fences,
nothing to keep the cows from drifting, and if a man was to do a
good job he had to constantly be watchin' and feelin' what the cows

were doin' and work behind any drift. Whistle could do that alright; he knew the country and how to work it.

Whistle had a passion for gatherin' every cow he could get his hands on, no matter how aggravating the situation. If a man happened to come into a holdup minus some cows he had started, chances were damn good that Whistle would take a few men and try to get around them a second time. He gave a cow brute every chance in the world to get to the holdup and then he always had his holdups set in good places, too. Low and behold if something should go through the middle of a holdup or break out of a herd! Whistle expected to gather cattle, not tell about them that got away. He savvied where things were gonna happen better'n any man I ever knew and he proved it by bein' there.

Coley Lyons tells me about Whistle when he was younger. "I loved to watch Whistle leave a holdup follerin' somethin' that had just broke out. I used to like to guess how long it would take him to catch it. I'd guess a number then start countin'. When I'd get to my number, I'd sing out, 'Make 'er bawl, Whistle!' And you know, I got purty good at guessin' the gentleman, too!

"When I first worked with Whistle," says Coley, "big bunches of cattle would scare Whistle purty bad, and he hated like hell to be too badly outnumbered. I remember one time, a long time ago, when we got a bunch of yearlin's and some old spoiled cows throwed together and finally got them held up, or kinda got 'em held up, like sayin', they're stopped for a while, anyway. Whistle knows we're purty badly outnumbered and he starts to fret and worry about how we're gonna move 'em. Like sayin', this is a long time ago and Whistle still hasn't figured out anyway to move livestock except to lead 'em!"

There come a time, though, when Whistle's job interfered with his passion to gather every last cow brute. It seems that Jim Walk, the R O's general manager, had been workin' with the wagon for a few days. Finally, one day, after Whistle had layed an ol' "get-away cow" down on her side just after she left the herd, Jim calls Whistle out of ear range of the rest of the men and tells him, "Whistle, you're just gonna have to quit puttin' your rope around the neck of every critter that sticks her head out of the roundup. It's just not good management. The boss has got to set an example for his men and the rest of these boys just can't rope like you. Why, it won't be long before we've got cowboys goin' in every direction followin' somethin' just a buildin' and a throwin', just a buildin' and a throwin'. I tell you, Whistle, it just don't look right for the boss of this here wagon to have somethin' on the end of his rope *all* the time!"

Whistle had a bad problem with whiskey along about this time. By the time I got to know him, though, he had quit drinkin' and seemed to even dislike talk about it. Back in the years we're talkin' about though, the jug had a purty strong holt on him and it nearly cost him his job.

Jim Walk could put up with a lot from Whistle 'cause he knew he could get the job done. But it was a thorn in Jim's side, and when he found he couldn't tell when Whistle was gonna be drunk and when he wasn't, it got to be more than he could stand. Then, too, how could he make an exception for Whistle and his drinkin' and then fire another man who was drinkin' but not a good enough hand to make a man want to put up with it? He finally decided he'd have to let him go.

Jim gives Whistle the word and he tells him to load his outfit in his pickup and he'd give him a ride into Prescott. When they get there, Jim allows as how he'd buy Whistle a drink. They're at the Palace Bar. There's other cowpunchers there that Jim hadn't seen in a while and that first shot led to another and it ain't long 'til Jim's forgot all about firin' Whistle! They end up closin' down the bar and they both think they got the world by the tail when they push through the

swingin' doors on the way out. They might'a been staggerin' but they think they're skippin' and there ain't nothin' these two ol' boys don't know! They're all smiles and neither remembers why they come to town.

Naturally, they take a quart with 'em, and after climbin' in the pickup, Whistle pulls the cork and tosses 'er out the window. Watchin' that cork bounce across the street Whistle throws back his head and squalls for the whole world to know how he feels! The way them ol' boys pass that bottle back and forth you'd'a thought they was about to die of thirst.

Jim starts out of town and they keep passin' that bottle of joy, each takin' his turn a tellin' the other how smart he is and what all he's done. It's been stormin', and the closer they get to the ranch, the worse the road gets. They make it about a mile from the bunkhouse when they bog 'er down right in front of Charlie Greene's (the owner's house)! They're in the middle of a big flat, and after sizin' up the situation, decide to tie onto Charlie's windmill tower with their winch. It's the only thing in sight and sure looks handy to these smilin' gents! Jim's drivin' a four-wheel-drive pickup, and when she finally stops, she's buried plumb to the frame.

When daylight comes, there's two passed-out cowpunchers, one empty bottle, one stuck pickup, and one windmill tower layin' on it's side to greet Charlie! Whistle tells me that Jim never mentioned his drinkin' again!

Cowboy manners were more than a way of life for Whistle; they were a religion, and as long as he ran a wagon, he made sure that everyone minded his manners. Cowpunchers love a laugh, and when someone (especially a boss) is as devoted to somethin' as strong as Whistle was to good cowboy manners, he lays himself wide open to someone's prank.

For a puncher to tend to his toiletries too close to the wagon is a cardinal sin. Even after takin' a good hike a man is expected to burn his toilet paper. This is all too obvious. With a strong wind blowin', toilet paper would be blowin' through camp, and no man likes to be squatted down enjoyin' his beef steak and frijoles and have a length of toilet paper wrap around his neck!

We were camped at Francis Creek one fall. The wagon was camped on one side of the creek and the horse corrals were on the other. It had been a number of years since a good flood had come through and the willows had grown purty thick. We had a narrow trail beat through 'em and an old plank layed across the water. The ol' boy that was the camp man at Francis Creek at that time had an old hound dog. This ol' dog was a regular ol' beggar, and as soon as the crew pulled out in the mornin', he'd slip across the creek and see what he could bum off the cook. Well, after one of these visits, this ol' flop-eared pot-licker stops in the middle of our trail and relieves himself in a large pile!

Now there's one cowpuncher in particular that's been waitin' to job Whistle for a long time. After jerkin' off his saddle, he heads for the wagon. When he spys this pile in the middle of the trail he dang near breaks his neck lookin' back over his shoulder to see if Whistle's comin'. Whistle's not in sight, and the next thing that appears is a wad of toilet paper poked neatly in the top of that dog's business! This feller's so tickled with hisself he dang near chokes hisself down tryin' to keep from laughin' out loud. The rest of the crew is right behind him and them that don't see him pull the paper are soon tipped off by them that are wise.

Everyone's hunkered down with a cup of coffee when Whistle crosses the water. All eyes are on him as he disappears in the brush; it's the calm before the storm.

Directly there's a beller from that brush that could be heard plumb to the top of Mahone Mountain! When Whistle come out, it didn't take a wizard to see he had a horn drooped. All eyes went straight to the ground as he come stridin' up the hill cussin' every step of the way. What Whistle was gonna do or say we'll never know, 'cause when he got to the wagon, three cowpunchers doubled over in laughter! It was all the rest of them could do to keep from rollin' on the ground themselves.

Whistle's head snapped up, and in wide-eyed disbelief, his mouth dropped open. A second before Whistle was so mad he could have bit hisself. Now, as he stared at this spectacle in front of him, he knew the joke was on him! Bein' the man he was, he took the job with a smile, stepped around the howlin' cowpunchers, and made his way to the coffee pot.

On Time

▼▼▼▼▼▼

Most cowpunchers I ever knowed never carried watches," says ol' Brushy. "If they did carry 'em, they was pocket watches, tucked away where they wouldn't get broke. These watches that a man straps to his wrist is sure in danger of gettin' broke awful easy. The only clock the old-time Indians used was the one that come up in the East and down in the West, and they seemed to get along just fine. After dark, they could keep purty close tabs on the time by watchin' the Big Dipper travel around the North Star. It's nearly a lost art by now but there's still a few ol' boys around the country that can do it yet.

"Cowboys ain't the highest paid labor in the world but there's damn few of 'em that would trade jobs with a clock-puncher no matter what the pay. There ain't nothing that throws fear into cowpunchers faster than a nine-to-five job. To be tied down by a clock is one thing they won't stand for. Cows and horses live by the sun and the weather; this makes cowpunchers do the same. Whether a man is gatherin' cows or just prowlin' amongst 'em makes no difference. He's got to be there, on time, as it's gettin' light. Cows are up movin' and grazin' as soon as they can see. The calves are with 'em or close by, as they're needin' some *leche* to fill their bellies, too. Within a couple of hours the calves are layin' down again, and mama is either workin' her way toward water or tryin' to rustle a little feed for her paunch, leavin' the little feller hid out in a bush, low place, or high clump of grass. Sometimes there'll be a babysitter with a bunch of calves. She'll stay with them little critters, watchin' over 'em, makin' sure no varmints disturbs 'em till one of the other mamas comes back from water; then she'll pull out for water herself, leavin' her calf behind. It's all instinct with 'em and a calf will never leave the place his mama has left him, and if he's run off the spot, he'll keep tryin' to go back to it. It's a sure enough safe bet that when an outfit gatherin' cattle starts jumpin' calves without their mothers, they are too late and they're goin' to miss a bunch of cattle, 'specially calves.

"No," says ol' Brushy, "there ain't no such thing as bein' too early on a cow outfit but you can sure as hell be too late! This bothers some of these city folks and college boys that seem to be buyin' and managin' cow outfits these days. Why, they nearly have a stroke when they go by some ol' boy's camp and he's got his feet up and a snorin' away in the middle of the afternoon. The thing they don't know is that this feller left camp when it was just light enough to see and he put in a full day's work before he got back to camp. He didn't have no coffee breaks or lunch hour either; he stayed till he got his work done and he's still got his evenin' chores to do!

"Some of these modern outfits have got to where they can stay under their bed tarps a little longer on account of they don't have to trot to their work but load their horses in a truck or trailer and haul to work. Even so, these outfits still got to be up and a ginnin' by the time it's light.

"You might not find one watch among a wagon crew," says ol' Brushy, "but you're sure to find an alarm clock and watch amongst the wagon boss's and cook's layout. These are two fellers that keep an outfit movin' and they need to be runnin' on time. It's a matter of pride to most cooks to holler chuck on time. Fact is, I see a cook try to quit one time 'cause he overslept and didn't have his steak fried till it was plumb daylight. He was ashamed to the point he thought he had to quit. The boss saw it different, though, 'specially since he needed a cook awful bad. After a few kind words, he talks this ol' bisquit-baker into staying. He ain't happy about the late start but he's still got a cook!

"That same boss got another late start one time," says ol' Brushy. "He's hired him another cook, as the other one quit between works. This one says he's worked all over the country but after hearing him talk, it's plain he's never worked for no big outfits, just small family ranches. This should've tipped his hand but the boss has got other things on his mind and don't see the writin' on the wall. I ain't got nothin' against small outfits, mind you," says ol' Brushy. "I reckon there's some sure enough good ones but some of these ain't under the pressure to get their work done that the big ones are. If the weather turns sour, lots of times they'll pull up and wait it out. They probably don't have but one man on the payroll; the rest of the crew is made up of family and neighbors.

·   "Well, the wagon pulls out and, sure enough, the first night out it rains. What I mean, it runs water all over, and come time for the cook to build a fire, it's still rainin'. The rattlin' of a dutch oven lid wakes the boss and when he throws his tarp back, daylight hits him square in the face! By the time he gets to the cook, he's as hot as the fire the cook is a pokin' at. He's not sayin' nothin', waitin' for the cook to make his play first. The cook greets him with a big rosy smile and, 'Good mornin', sure a good rain last night!' *Now* he's mad and he figures anything he says right now ain't gonna be right, so he just grunts out, 'Mornin'' and waits for the coffee to boil. After the coffee boils and he drinks a cup, he explains to the cook about the breakfast bein' at the time he say's it'll be, no matter what the weather and such things as leavin' runnin' of the outfit up to him. He now savvies this ol' boy ain't worked for no big outfits but tells me later, 'I don't know how much ol' Cookie learns from the lecture that mornin' but I sure learned one thing, and the next time I went to headquarters, I got me an alarm clock and it's been in my outfit ever since.'

"Some outfits," says ol' Brushy, "just run too smooth to suit some fellers. I wasn't there but I hear about such a time on the Bar Cross outfit. The outfit is run by Paul Moore. He's a small man but everyone respects him 'cause he's a good boss and knows how to handle his job. The cook is an ol' cowpuncher with a build plumb opposite that of Paul. He stands better than six feet and has just enough meat on his bones to let you know he ain't died yet. Like Paul, he knows his job too. They got a good crew and the work is going smooth, or as one feller thought, too smooth.

"When someone likes their job like these two fellers liked their job it's a cinch that they're gonna do a good job and have a lot of pride in the way they do it. As humble as they might have been, they couldn't help themselves to brag now and then about how the work was goin'. One thing these fellers had in common was that they was sure proud of the way they got the crew a goin' in the mornin'. Paul liked to remind the crew every few days how *this* outfit *always* left

camp with a jar, same way ol' Cookie liked to remind everyone that the chuck was *always* on time.

"There was a big overgrown kid in the crew. He wasn't the best hand in the country but what he lacked in knowledge he made up for in energy. It seems his energy wasn't just in his big frame but in his head too. I reckon he got tired of hearin' these two fellers brag on how they got out of bed so early and decides it's time to lower them back to earth. The idear strikes him when he notices both Paul and the cook have alarm clocks in their beds. The kid is sly and nobody sees him when he deals out the trick.

"Next mornin' the crew is woke to a screamin', pot bangin' fit goin' on by the fire. Paul has got a fire goin'; the cook is still in bed and it's plain that Paul ain't about to let him enjoy any extra winks under his bed tarp. The next thing the crew knows, ol' Cookie has got his alarm in his hand and clad only in his long handles he's marchin' toward the fire! All he lacks is the bellerin', or he'd look like a bull goin' to battle. Under every bed tarp two eyes are a peerin' out at the fire. When they square off, the fire's between 'em but they're puffed up and got their chins stuck out and they come damn near bumpin' heads. Paul's still a cussin' and has got a pot hook raised over his head. It don't slow Cookie none and he shoves his alarm clock at Paul's belly and pointin' at it with a long skinny finger, screeches, 'Look at this, you dumb son of a bitch, it says 2:30. That means I got an hour before I build a fire! *You* better get the hell outta my kitchen or *you're* gonna be the new cook around here!'

"Paul's jaw gapes open and with the fire right under him he sure looks wild-eyed and scary. Whirlin' away from the fire, he stomps to his bed and gets his clock. When he gets back to the fire, he shoves it in ol' Cookie's face and hollers, '*You're* the son of a bitch! Look at this, it's 4:30 and *you're* an hour late!' They're still squared off across the fire; Paul's still a wavin' his pot hook and the cook's a standin' straddle-legged in his long johns, lookin' down at Paul and still a pointin' and a screechin' at the top of his lungs. The crew figures they're about to witness murder when, of a sudden, they both go quiet, and turnin', they both stare out into the darkness where the cowpunchers are a peekin' at this strange spectacle. It's quiet a while, then Paul finally manages to stammer out, 'I-i-i-if I e-e-ever find out who done this, I promise, I-I-I-I'll kill the sorry sucker!'

"The crew that was there swears they never, ever even seen a late start on that outfit!"

■ ▪ ▪ ▪ ▪ ▪ ▪ ▪

THE
REAL
WEST

Romance of
the West

▼▼▼▼▼▼

I've heard tell that most folks 'low as how cowpunchers are about
half-locoed," says ol' Brushy, "and I reckon as how they're half-
right. But, I'll tell ya that if it weren't for cowpunchers, there'd
be a lot less beef steak for them city folks to eat. Most of them city
folks think that all it takes to be a cowboy is to wear a hat and boots.
Fact is, they think real cowpunchers are extinct.

"I was in town not long ago, gassin' up at a filling station when
a carload pulls up from New York. There was a man and his wife,
five kids, and a little poodle dog crammed into a station wagon that
had suitcases tied on top. As soon as the car come to a halt, the doors
flew open and the kids and dog came a boilin' out, a shoutin' and
a runnin'.

"The old man was a wearin' a matchin' getup of flowered short-
sleeved shirt and shorts that hung halfway to his knees. He's got low-
cut shoes and socks with little red hearts on 'em that reach up to his
knees. His belly tells me he don't do nothin' much tougher than pull
the trigger on his camera that he's got hung around his neck.

"The woman is the last to get out, as she's been a fussin' with
her hairdo and makeup, but when she does climb out for her ap-
pearance, she starts right in a screamin' at the kids, 'Come *back here*
Sally!' and 'Oh, Johnny, when will you learn not to get so dirty!' and
'Tommy stay away from that filthy horse!' (Tommy had spotted the
horse in the back of my truck.)

"Then it happens. The whole bunch seems to spot me all at once and they all come a lookin' with jaws gaping. They really look me over, from head to foot, takin' the whole thing in. They ain't never seen anything as ridiculous as this. From my hat, to my long-sleeved shirt, to my Levis and high-heeled boots, they take it all in. Finally, one of the little boys asks, 'Are you a cowboy, Mister!'

"At which the father takes over, 'Don't be silly Samuel, he's just a farm hand. There aren't any real cowboys anymore!'

"These kind of people only know about cowpunchers what they read, and since most of what they read is romantic fairy tales about the West, they just naturally think that it's a bunch of bull. They reason that there just ain't no more cowboys 'cause the Injuns is all on reservations and there ain't no more trail herds on the way to Abeline.

"A friend of mine tells me a story about his wife. It seems she went to town to do her monthly shoppin' and has a conversation with another woman she runs into. After visitin' for a spell, the talk gets around to their husbands and what they do for a livin'. When asked what her husband does, my friend's wife replies, 'He's a cowboy.' At which the lady just kind of smiles an unbelievin' smile as if to just humor her newfound acquaintance. She goes on, 'He's on the wagon right now, so I haven't seen him for nearly a month.' At this, the other lady shook her head and patting my friend's wife on the hand said very sincerely, 'Oh, you poor, poor dear! When will these men ever learn to grow up? Tsk, Tsk, can you just imagine, playing cowboy and probably carousing in bars until they're alcoholics? Can you just imagine? On the wagon. Oh, you poor, poor dear!'

"The romance of the West has held on a long time but a good friend of mine, Tom Almond, has a hard time seeing the romance.

"Me and Tom was trottin' back to camp one day when a sure enough thunder storm caught us. Big black clouds begin boilin' up in the southeast; lightning started poppin' around us and then come the rain! It was one of those storms a man remembers the rest of his life. Seconds later we was both drenched; you couldn't see a dozen feet down the trail and it was cold, too! Pretty quick it turned to hail about the size of your thumbnail; in an instant water was running everywhere. It had been a dry booger with lots of dry tanks, so we was both grinnin' from ear to ear, but a cold soakin' like that has a way of wipin' the smile off a man's face. The trail we was travelin' followed a high malapai rim and it seemed like the lightning was going to usher us off that high country. Each time it cracked it was a

little closer, makin' the hair stand straight up on the
back of my neck. It'll sober a man up right quick
and remind him how little he is.
When we finally got off
the rim, we both felt
a little safer but
the rain and
hail kept com-
ing in sheets.

"The trail wound down through the boulders and cedar trees. Tom was still traveling as fast as he could, but this country's not fast when it's dry, and now our ol' ponies are having a hard time keeping on their feet. The wind is blowing hard when we slide to the bottom of the canyon. Tom pulls up, and squinting out from under my hat, I look to see what makes Tom stop so suddenly. The water is a rollin' down the canyon, and above the roar of the storm, we could hear the boulders being mashed and rolled along!

" 'End of the trail!' Tom shouts, grinnin' out from under his sagging hat brim. Backing into a cedar tree and away from the wind, we know we've got a long wait. After we'd been humped up for what seemed forever, the storm finally begins to weaken. Tom never wasted words and this wasn't no exception. He said it all when he shivered out, 'Kinda takes the romance out of punchin' cows, don't it?'

"Hell, that's just one story," says Brushy. "The life of a cow-puncher is full of such times. If it ain't rain, hail, and lightning it's snow, ice, and freezing cold, or mud, or dust so thick you can't see or breathe, or wind mixed with any of 'em. How about a drought, dry and hot, no feed and no water? There ain't nothin' as tryin' as to move a bunch of poor starved cows that's been hung up at a dry tank. The calves ain't nothin' but hairballs and it takes a hand to tell which of these little fellers is doggies and which ain't!

"How about shoeing horses? There's always that pony that's waitin' for you to get careless, or the one that won't even let you get past his shoulder without trying to rearrange your skeleton. You try to be patient 'cause you know you never get nowhere fightin' a horse, but after tryin' every trick you know and hearin' all the advice from the cowboys watchin', you end up doing what you knew you was gonna do in the beginning: tie him down! You finally get iron nailed on him all the way around knowing damn well that he'll probably be the first horse in your mount to throw a shoe, 'cause it's hard to do a good job standing on your head! By the time you get finished, both you and your horse are wringin' with sweat; but when you let him up, you want to cry, 'cause strainin' against the ropes, he's crippled hisself and you know it's gonna be a while before you can ride him!

"Ever since the birth of the cowboy there's been authors that's tried to paint an image of a hard-ridin', fast-shootin' hombre in a white hat that's out to win the West. They very seldom face the fact that these boys work on horseback. It ain't all fun and glamour.

"It kinda takes the romance outta punchin' cows when a water gap goes out and a man spends the best part of a day packing wire, post, axe, shovel, or whatever he needs on a mule (and most mules don't like the job any better than the cowpuncher and ain't too proud to prove it!); it's not pleasant work but it's got to be done. But the smile of a job well done fades to cussin' when, headed back to camp, the cowpuncher looks over his shoulder and sees a big black thunderhead emptying it's belly out just above his new water gap. The only thing that keeps this puncher from throwin' a first-class tantrum is that he knows the country sure needs the rain and without it there just ain't no romance at all.

"I reckon there's no such thing as a perfect job but I'll bet there's nothin' quite as disagreeable to a cowpuncher as calving a bunch of two-year-old heifers. There's always been disagreement on the pros and cons of breeding yearling heifers and those that are for it are strickly speaking about economics (and there's plenty of room for argument there). It's a sure bet, though, that you won't find many cowpunchers in favor of it.

"Cowpunchers work too hard and take too much pride in taking care of livestock they been put in charge of to be in favor of somethin' that puts their cows in danger. I ran into Lloyd Hodges a few years ago after he just finished calving out a bunch of two-year-old heifers. He was still stirred up; I guess all the dead calves and broke-down heifers had pretty well got to him. He finished up his tirade by sayin', 'They ought to make it a law that any son of a bitch who gives the order to breed a yearling heifer has got to pull every calf, lick it off, and eat the afterbirth!'

"Romance!" says Brushy. "Why, all the romance I get comes out of a paperback written by some dude back East that ain't never seen a cowboy! It makes for mighty good readin' on a cold winter's night, though; them fellers sure got a good imagination!"

Bold Knights
of the Saddle

▼▼▼▼▼▼▼

I've been tamped full of BS about cowboys,
known as the wild and romantic band.
Bold knights of the saddle,
That roundup wild cattle,
And roll a cigarette with one hand.

(ANONYMOUS)

Yup," ol' Brushy says, "accordin' to movies and fiction, he's a sheik in a ten-gallon hat! But I never have figured out where the authors of these Wild West paperbacks, pulp magazines, and movies get their stuff. Why, they got the common people believin' that us cowpunchers are as romantic as a bottle of French champagne in the moonlight!" Ol' Brushy goes on. "The ol' boy they got dolled up in a white hat and shirt, sittin' on the top rail of the corral at the home ranch, pickin' a guitar and swoonin' the purty widow while the sun goes down and just waitin' for a range war to break out is somewhat different than what I see hired out to this outfit! Them fellers that ride white horses and can shoot another feller off a black horse at about a quarter-mile away is plumb different to some of these shootin' exhibitions put on by cowpunchers at a butcherin'!

"These silver-tongued woman-killers in movin' pictures have sure enough got their lines put together. Why, if they could talk to a cow as smooth as they talk to women, they could talk a cow out of her calf, and she'd never even bawl! Not that sure enough cowboys ain't polite, they're that alright, 'specially if you think polite is a mute with a silly grin on his mug that's hung down in embarrassment, shiftin' from one leg to the other and his ol' rough paws rollin' up the brim of his new Stetson (somethin' he'd kill someone else for doin' to his new hat).

"While our hero rides into the valley and leads the poor widow's rag-tag bunch of ranch hands into warfare with the wealthy, land-greedy Cattle Baron, the cowpuncher I know is probably ridin' some limber-necked bronc down some canyon so rough it'd make a mountain goat turn back and leadin' a hard-tail loaded down with salt.

"Both these gents are in a battle alright, but one's just not as romantic as the other. The ol' boy in the movies is in a shoot-out that lasts anywhere from five to ten hours (they don't never run out of ammunition) and ends up with our hero in a horse race with the bad guy. Our man finally overtakes the villain and bull-dogs him.

They rolls to the bottom of the hill where the durndest fist fight you ever seen takes place (this lasts for a good ten minutes). Finally, our man gets winded and decides to pull his six-shooter, partin' the bad hombre's hair with his Colt .45 and bringin' the range war to an end! When he gets back to the purty little wider, she's all over him, askin' if he's alright and a kissin' and a huggin' him. Outside of a little dust he knocks off his sombrero, you couldn't have told that he'd done nothin' but pick lillies and his guitar all day!"

Ol' Brushy stops just long enough to catch his air and bite off some more Brown's Mule, then says, "Like I said, I don't know where them fellers gets their information, 'cause the ol' boy we left packin' salt down the canyon don't match up no way with that gun-totin', silver-stamped warrior of the West. Oh, our puncher was doin' battle alright, but it wasn't near as romantic! He's all by hisself, outside of his bronc and mule, and goin' down the bottom of this canyon where the rocks and brush are so bad (this ol' boy claims that this is where the trail ends and the West begins) his bronc gets to grabbin' hisself and showin' the whites of his eyes. Every time they go through some brush (and that's purty often, since a jackrabbit couldn't turn around here without losin' some hair) Mr. Bronc blows them rollers in his nose and drops his off ear. The cowpuncher knows it ain't long till this cayuse is goin' to try to widen the trail.

"People that say mules ain't smart ain't never been around 'em, and this mule ain't no exception. This hard-tail has packed salt like an angel for the last two years, just waitin' for such a moment as this! Blowin' his nose like a wild mustang, the mule tries to go by the bronc on the near side. 'Course he makes sure the lead rope goes under the tail as he goes by and he rams the salt that's hung on his off side into the butt of the bronc! This opens the battle for our cowpuncher. Naturally, his dallies foul and he ain't able to get rid of his mule; this battleground's not as big as the one in the paperback but it gets bigger all the time. The bronc is squeelin' and bawlin', and this cowpuncher thinks that if he did get bucked off right now, this ol' pony might just eat him right there! The dallies come loose just before the lead rope wipes the cowboy out of the saddle but not before that pack turns and scatters the salt, leavin' the pack saddle under the mule's belly and a broke britchen! Them first few jumps this outlaw makes, the cowboy thinks is easy; but when the mule come loose, he sees it's just the mule that's been keepin' him so close to earth! Now that

this pony don't have to take the mule with him, he starts for the moon. The next jump the cowboy claims he gets a bloody nose; he don't know whether it was the sudden change in altitude or if it was the branch that he tries to tear off of a tree with his face as they go by. Either way, he starts to get a little dizzy and his head is a poppin' by now and he's about to go blind. He don't feel like no hero and he's tryin' to hold on to anything he can grab, but his grip gets weak, and where he does find somethin' to hang onto, it just gets jerked loose again. By this time he's beggin' the pony to stop but the hoss ain't got no more conscience than the mule and each jump gets a little stouter. By the time the puncher comes loose, he's still thinkin' clear enough to hang onto his McCarty that's stuffed through his belt. He hangs on for all his worth, but the battle ends when he tries to pulverize a boulder with his head, partin' his hair right down to his skull. He sees stars for a while, but when he comes to, he sees he's all alone, except for four salt blocks that's scattered around this little open flat that he's layin' in! He can't remember no open flat in this canyon and thinks maybe he's dreamin'; but surveyin' the area, he remembers it's his hoss and the mule that clears the brush and boulders all around him!

"It's a long walk home for this skinned-up cowboy. Both his horse and mule are waitin' at the back gate of the horse pasture, and though they snort and blow as he walks up, they both takes the gate when he opens it and steps back.

"When he gets back to camp, he ain't got no purty wider lady to nurse his wounds and sew his shirt back together for him. These things he's got to do for hisself, and as for pity, he gets that from his partner that shares this camp, who says 'By God, Pard, your gettin' ta where ya can't ride nothin'!' "

ROPES
AND
ROPIN'

Ropes

▼▼▼▼▼

In the book *Trails Plowed Under,* Charlie Russell says, "Ropes, like guns, are dangerous. All the difference is, guns go off and ropes go on." Ol' Charlie knew more and could tell and paint more about the old time cowpuncher than any man before or since his time and he sure never missed a lick on ropes. He painted and told about some wrecks that will make the hair stand up on the back of your neck. But there's been many a wreck since his time, and as long as cowpunchers is packin' ropes, there's gonna be many more. There ain't a cowboy alive that could look you in the eye and say he's never been in some kind of wreck with a rope.

It's a funny thing, cowpunchers ain't the most cautious critters on this earth and even ol' Charlie partrayed 'em as a wild and reckless breed. Now, it just don't make sense that the employers of these kind would furnish them with somethin' as dangerous as a gun, but that's what they do. Sure enough, they furnish these woolies with ropes and expect 'em to use 'em too!

I reckon that the rope is the single most important tool the cowboy uses. Many a time I've heard some puncher say how plumb naked he felt if he had lost his rope somehow and had to finish out the day without it.

The cowpuncher's day starts out with catchin' his horse and more times than not he hoolihans him out of the remuda. If it's a southern outfit and one or two men do all the horse catchin', chances are good that the rest of the crew have made a corral out of their ropes to hold the remuda, each man throwin' the end of his rope to the man on his right until a circle has been made.

If an outfit is workin' in the spring, calves get drug to the brandin' fire on the end of a rope. 'Course any kind of a cow brute that don't take to such activities and don't show an interest in joinin' the roundup is generally persuaded by a cowpuncher and his rope.

The camp man, workin' and prowlin' his country alone, has plenty of use for his rope, too. Pinkeye, lice, horns growed into heads, and footrot are some of the most common reasons a cowboy has of

catchin' a cow brute. There's still an outbreak of screw worms every few years in the Southwest or maybe a prolapsed cow that needs sewin' up, too. Then too, there's still some outfits that range brand.

In the fall, calves that were missed in the spring or born too late for the spring works have to be branded. Most of these big ol' calves are head and heeled.

In a country where there's lots of wild cattle, you can bet that a cowboy known as a "wild cow man" is mighty handy with a catch rope. He savvies the wild cow and knows how she thinks. He'll try to gather her first and use every bit of knowledge he's gained in a lifetime of followin' these ol' Suzies; but when hell breaks loose and there's no other way, you can bet he's got his rope down and it ain't long till she's tied to a tree!

Most every outfit I ever worked for handles horses different, but it's a cinch that no matter how different these methods are they all use a rope.

Brandin' weaner colts, some outfits catch 'em around the neck and then a couple of cowboys go down the rope and mug the colt, wrestlin' him to the ground. Other outfits may head and heel 'em.

Most outfits cut the stud colts at two years of age but right there is where the similarity stops. Some head and heel 'em, some fore foot 'em, and some catch 'em around the neck and then fore foot 'em. Anyway, they all get the job done and they all use ropes.

Now when a man goes to start a bronc it's a sure bet he don't step in the round corral with a handful of sugar and a mouthful of baby talk. He'll be skakin' out a loop as he goes through the gate and whether he catches him ahorseback or afoot or whether he catches him around the neck or fore foots him doesn't make much difference; that's up to the man doin' the work. What does make a difference is that this man's packin' a rope and he's gonna have aholt on this bronc purty quick.

There's not a day goes by that a cowpuncher doesn't use his rope, even if just to shut a gate. That rope gets to be a part of him, and if you was to take it away, it would be like cuttin' off his arm!

Ol' Brushy tells about a job he takes down on the Mexican border by the town of Sasabe, Arizona. "Now," Brushy starts in, "this outfit works straight Mexicans straight out of Old Mexico and me and the general manager are the only gringos on the payroll. The manager don't work with us but gives his pills to his *jefe*.

"There's parts of the cow business that these ol' boys from the south ain't learned yet, like motherin' cows and calves up after movin' them from one pasture to another or how to work a herd; but when it comes to usin' a reata, there's not much these fellers don't savvy.

"I ain't been there long," says Brushy, "when one of these beaners says he's located a beehive and calls on the rest of us to help him rob it. The hive is a hangin' from the eve of an old rundown shack. Gettin' an old oil drum and rollin' it up under the hive, they pile cow chips on top of it and set 'em on fire to make a smoke.

"They all head for cover (me in the lead) 'cept one of 'em who's volunteered to stand under the hive and keep the flames beat down with a gunny sack so as to make a sure enough good smudge. I expect," claims Brushy, "that everything would have went to plan, if it hadn't been for a slight breeze that comes up about this time and the smoke never quite makes it to the hive! These bees are a curious bunch and are plenty anxious to investigate what this chili-eater is doin' buildin' fires and wavin' his arms so close to their hacienda! When poor ol' Pedro sees these bees have taken such a keen interest in him, he throws up his hands and starts a hookin' it across the country so fast that he's got the brim of his sombrero flattened up against the crown. Every jump he's a screamin' at the top of his lungs, '*Dame mi' reata!* (Give me my rope!) '*Dame me' reata!*' "

Brushy 'lows as how he had no idear what this ol' boy was gonna do with his reata, but it sure showed that he had lived with a rope in his hand for so long that when things got tight, his reata was the first thing he thought of!

I think that purty well tells the story. A sure enough cowpuncher is helpless without his rope, and without his rope, he just ain't a cowpuncher!

Experimentin'

⬛⬜⬛⬜⬛⬜⬛

A kid raised on the range is purty near to bein' born with a rope in his hand. From the time one of these little buttons can travel on his hind feet, he starts imitatin' the cowpunchers he sees about the ranch. One of the first things you see these little fellers do is to pick up a string or light rope and go to swingin' it. By the time this waddie is about four years old, he's got every dog, cat, and chicken on the place rope-shy and sleepin' with one eye open. It comes natural to him, and after he gets old enough to follow dad around on horseback he gets the urge to start experimentin' to see what he can and can't get done by his lonesome. It don't even start to enter his head that Dad has a lifetime of experience on him, and when he sees Dad crackin' his nylon on some ol' cow, layin' a trip on her, puttin' ol' Suzie on the ground, and tiein' her there—it looks so easy!

Well, it ain't long till he's sneakin' off by hisself and gainin' that experience he'll need later on to make hisself useful.

Some time ago there was a cowboy and his family stayin' at the Tubs camp on Babbitt's C O Bar Ranch. This feller had a boy named John, who was gettin' to the age where he's got to do some of this experimentin'.

The boss has asked John to take care of a few doggies that the cowpunchers have picked up. 'Course this tickles John and he ain't long in accepting the offer that the boss makes him.

John keeps his doggies in the horse pasture, gathering them in the evenings and shutting them up overnight, feeding them both at evening and in the morning. Now, John's stuck names on all his calves and one of 'em is Big Boy. He gets his name 'cause he don't fit the rest of the doggies; fact is, you could hardly call him a doggie. He's an early calf and was plenty big enough to wean already; only reason he ended up in the bunch was because somewhere along the way while mov- ing the cows to the summer country, he had lost his mama and so the handiest thing to do with him was to put him in with the doggies.

Well, one evening, while gathering his doggies, John is, naturally, playing with his rope. It's not long till he decides to try something, so crowdin' his ol' pony up on Big Boy, he just sticks it on him! Now, he's not tied hard, so takin' his dallies he gets the outfit stopped.

Right here is where his little ol' brain is startin' to work overtime! Who would have thought that gentle ol' Big Boy would cause such a fuss! The way Big Boy is a jumpin' it's a cinch that it's not gonna be as easy as he figured. Oh well, he'd seen Dad go down the rope to a calf many a time, so why couldn't he?

He's got a horn knot in the end of his rope but when he turns his dallies loose to put it on his horn, Big Boy leaves there, trying to catch the other doggies that have long since headed for the feed trough. John spurs up, but while he's a puttin' his horn knot on, he forgets about his slack and his horse runs up over it! Getting his horn knot on, John sets his pony — and the wreck is on! When the rope comes tight, it's over the top of John's leg, down under his pony's belly, and then out between his hind legs! John says later that the rope has purty well got him tied on, and from what he says this ol' cowhorse does, it's the only way he could have rode him! Things finally come undone and everything gets straight. John's sure glad of that, but he don't know that his education has just begun.

Goin' down the rope, just like he's seen them other punchers do it, he figures he'll make short work of the rest of the project. But Big Boy has different ideas; by now his eyes have plumb glazed over and with his tongue wallered out he comes up the rope a meetin' John, bellering all the way. He flattens this little puncher and keeps a goin'. By the time John gets up, Big Boy changes directions and runs over John a goin' the other way.

Now this ain't exactly the way John had the whole thing figured out, but now he's more than just a little ruffled himself, and if Big Boy is determined to get away, then John is just as determined to get him turned loose!

Big Boy makes a run at the horse, and when he makes a pass at the ol' pony, he picks up a hind leg again in the slack. Well, when things finally get still again, Big Boy is choked down on the end of the rope and John's horse is sittin' on his rear end, rope run down by his flank and out between his hind legs.

First, John thinks that if he could push his horse over, that would make enough slack, so things might straighten out! He's got a good idear, but since this pony outweighs him by nine hundred fifty pounds, it don't work!

He finally gets his fingers worked under the rope at Big Boy's neck, and tuggin' and pullin', he gets Big Boy drug far enough up to turn him loose! He says it takes Big Boy a while to get his air!

School's out for the day, and John's learned more in the last few minutes than anyone could possibly ever preach to him about ropes and ropin'! I believe the good Lord watches over these little fellers while giving them experience they will need later on.

A Texas Wreck

■▬▬▬▬▬▬▬■

Boots O'neal tells me a while back, "If you'll think about it a while, there's not many wrecks that take place that don't have a rope in it somehow." Boots has worked for the J A's and Matador's and used to run the Waggoner Ranch in Texas. I figure he's seen a bunch of wrecks and knows what he says. He tells me a story that takes place not too long ago on the Waggoner Ranch.

"This ol' kid is about as woolie as they come; he was raised right there on the ranch and he ain't afraid of nothin'. He's got a purty tough mount of horses, but he never thinks about 'em; fact is, I don't think he ever knows it. He don't fear nothin' that wears hair, and when he starts out to do a job, he ain't about to let some horse's reputation get in his way."

Boots says, "We were roundin' a pasture when a big steer turns back and dives for the mesquites. This kid was onto Mr. Steer's hole card and has his rope down. He rolls the iron under his ol' pony, and standin' up in his stirrups and leanin' as far as he can, he reaches and ropes the steer right at the end of his rope! When things come tight, this ol' pony's head has already disappeared and he's bawlin' and tearin' up the earth. The kid proves he's a rider, 'cause he rides him. This time, though, it might have been better if he hadn't, 'cause this man-eater jumps up the rope, throwin' a bunch of slack in it then spins twice, wrapping the cowboy around the middle. Naturally, he's tied hard and fast in true Texas fashion! When the rope comes tight again, it jerks the cowboy out of the saddle about five feet and hangs him there. His horse ain't slowed down none and every time he jumps it nearly cuts this cowboy in two.

"These cowboys see the wreck and ride to help him. One of 'em dives off and cuts the rope between the cowboy and the steer, thinking that the cowboy would roll out of the rope. But, the rope has fouled and now that the steer has been turned loose, this outlaw starts to cover some country! The rope is just long enough to where the cowboy is right underneath this pony every jump and he's tryin' to do as much damage as he can."

Boots claimed there wasn't no way to rope this livin' piece of hell 'cause he still had his head buried between his front legs. The cowboy being drug has a brother, and he's one of the three that came to help. Well, his brother ain't long in sizin' up the situation, and diving off in bull-dog fashion right down amongst them feet, he comes up with a mouthful of ear and a thumb in the eye! This slows the ol' pony down enough where one of the other cowboys cuts his brother loose!

The cowboy lives but he's unconscious for thirteen days and suffers more than one broken bone!

By the time Boots tells me all of this, the cowboy is mendin' and startin' to ride again, and you can bet he's still packin' a rope, too, 'cause he's a cowpuncher and he'd feel just plumb naked without it!

BOOZE

Jerky Turns
Barkeep

▼▼▼▼▼▼

It had been cold and wet all fall. Huddled up in the cook tent, outta the sleet that was comin' down, one of the boys says, "I hadn't pulled my socks off for two weeks but last night I pulled 'em off and I swear I thinks I'm startin' to grow webs between my toes!" Another feller snorts and says, "Hell, Jake, you ain't growin' webs between your toes 'cause only ducks got webbed feet and in order to turn into a duck you gotta have wings. I'm here to tell ya, you ain't angel enough to sprout wings! Besides, it's too damn cold for ducks, they done went south a month ago."

"Hells fire, Pard, you're a fine one to talk," counters Jake. "When you pull off yer shirt tonight you oughta look over yer shoulder and see if you got any hair startin' to grow. An ol' coyote like you ought to be puttin' on your winter coat by now!"

"I don't know about the rest of you fellers," says Tank Morris, "but it's weather like this, that what makes me think about doin' somethin' else fer a livin'. Didn't ya ever wonder what it'd be like to sleep under a solid roof that don't leak and work next to a big pot-bellied stove that don't never cool off? Or maybe ride in a Cadillac to work instead of a bronc that would just as soon strike yer head off or maybe unload ya and make ya walk?"

Jerky Smith listens to this talk fer a while then real thoughtful like he unloads with a story that makes believers outta all of us. "I been travelin' a lot," says Jerky, "and puttin' my last five dollars in the gas tank of my old Ford, I makes 'er as far as the Palace Bar in Prescott. Steppin' into this cool oasis I strike up a conversation with Schell Dunbar, the owner of this waterin' hole. I tell him I'm lookin' for work but have run out of funds. He makes me an offer of a room in his hotel above the bar and board, too, for doin' some swampin' for him. He tells me that sooner or later every cowman in the country comes in there and it won't be long till I'm ahorseback again.

"It's the best offer I've had in quite a spell, so sheddin' my sombrero and washin' up my hands, I slick down my locks and grabbin' a towel I start to polishin' the old mahogany.

"Like I said, I'm a stranger in the country, but the way ol' Schell treats me, you'd 'a thought I was born and raised in his backyard. He's as right as rain in July and it ain't long before he's teachin' me how to build all them fancy drinks. So turnin' in my broom and mop I start pourin' whiskey. I've poured lots of whiskey in my time but it had always gone down my gullet; this time it's goin' into glasses! Things are goin' smooth as puddin', and bein' as the weather never changed in there and the pay is good, I'm thinkin' about quitin' the cowboy game and makin' a career outta this booze business. 'Course some mornings it's hard to climb from under the blankets, but after I've mixed a drink or two and sampled some of my wares, my head kind of limbers up and the soreness leaves. I'm mighty conscientious about my work, and bein' I ain't one to hand a man a bad drink, I feels it's my duty to sample each one before I hands it over the bar.

"I'm feelin' mighty fine most of the time and can't understand

this loss of weight that I'm experiencin'. Schell and I talk it over once and he claims some solid food would do wonders for me. I never was one to take much advice, always feelin' that firsthand experience was the best teacher, so I keep on gettin' my vitamins outta this bottled corn. I'm sure havin' a good time at my new profession but then I start to havin' a lapse of memory and can't never remember puttin' myself to bed for about three nights running. The mornin' after that last night, I'm downstairs pourin' breakfast when ol' Schell walks in. Says he, 'Jerky, I want you to know that you've sure been a big help to me and you've sure kept everyone entertained and full of whiskey, but there was a feller in here last night looking for a cowpuncher. I'd'a woke you up but you looked so damned comfortable stretched out there behind the bar I thought I would just let you sleep. Besides, I was afraid this feller might ask for your name and bein' a friend of yours, I didn't want you to be embarrassed by not bein' able to tell him! You done drank up your paycheck but here's some gas money,' he says handin' me five dollars. 'Oh, one other thing,' adds Schell. 'There's a pot sittin' on the stove in the back room. That black stuff that's in it is called coffee. Try some. You probably won't like it at first but stay with it; it kinda grows on a fella!'

"Steppin' outside, the bright sunlight nearly drives my eyes plumb to the back of my head. It makes me dizzy fer a minute, but leanin' agin' a parkin' meter, I finally gets my legs to workin'. They're mighty wobbly but I do manage to make 'er around the corner to where I'd left the ol' Ford tethered.

"My new boss is just as big hearted as ol' Schell, and usin' some of his own whiskey, he weans me off the joy juice real slow. In a couple weeks I'm back on full feed and startin' to get my strength back.

"Well, boys, there may be some of you try workin' at some new profession, but as fer me, I've had my whirl at that other world and I'll tell a man I'm plumb content right here!"

Spooks

I reckon it was the weather that got us to talkin' about spooks that night. The wind was a screamin' outside the bunkhouse, carrying with it spurts of snow that came every little bit. Every few minutes the old shack would moan under the strain of the wind and I guess one story led to another till we all had the hair on our necks standin' straight up.

"Talkin' about ghosts," says Pat, "puts me to mind of the time me and Mike camped at the old Asso camp north of the 'Frisco Peaks. It's a winter day, whole lot like this one. The wind is a whistlin' and the snow was a comin' in little flurries just coverin' the ground with a skiff. Only difference was, it was cold! The mercury had plumb buried itself for the past four days. We'd tried to ride the last three days but wasn't gettin' much done. The cattle was all humped up against the storm. It was one of them storms that northern Arizona is so famous for: lots of cold wind and not much moisture! On the fourth day we decides to chop ice and call 'er a day.

"We no more than had got back to camp, and while I was stokin' the stove and Mike was makin' a fresh pot of coffee, we heard some-one 'haloo the house! Goin' to the door Mike sees two fellers in a light buggy. They was braced against the storm with their hats tied down and their necks pulled down into their coats. The whole outfit was plastered with snow on the windy side. Mike spies a curious lookin' thing ridin' between these two fellers. The bottom rests on the floor board and the middle leans on the back of the seat, the top reaching a couple feet above the heads of these two fellers, all wrapped in canvas.

" 'Turn your horse loose in the corral and come in,' shouts Mike.

"When they come in, the biggest of the two introduces hisself and his partner as deputies from Flagstaff. They have been up to the Grand Canyon to pick up the body of a man that had been killed in an accident. Mike and I see right off that neither of these lawmen are too high on the job of haulin' bodies around!

"Well, we had a purty good start on the coffee pot when I breaks out one of the two bottles of whiskey that we have been savin' for such days as this. Everyone has warmed considerable with this joy juice running through us and our guests start thinking about pulling out for Flag. About this time, Mike allows as how he has some chores to do and heads out to the barn. I know Mike ain't got a damn thing to do at the barn, but figure he's got a right to play out his hand, so I don't call him.

"I try to talk the deputies into stayin' the night but I can't build a good enough case to argue with the whiskey that's got aholt of 'em. By this time, they're the toughest lawmen west of the Mississippi and there ain't no little ol' storm gonna keep 'em from travelin' when they want to travel! I stake 'em to what's left of the quart 'cause they got a long, cold trip ahead of 'em whether they know it or not.

"They ain't been gone out to the barn longer than ten minutes, when all of a sudden, they both come bustin' through the door. Both of 'em has lost their rosy glow of a few minutes before and are white as a sheet, and for as warm as they were, now their teeth are chattering, and about all I can understand when they try to talk is that they'd changed their minds and if the offer still stood they'd spend the night.

"Mike is just a few minutes behind these badge-toters, and when I see the look on his face, I'm satisfied that he's the reason behind the sudden change in plans!

"Next morning Mike is bouncing around happy as a lark, rearing to get a goin'. After we finish the breakfast dishes we all go out to the barn. Mike is still a whistlin' and a singin' and I know it ain't just 'cause the wind died during the night. No sir, he's been up to something. I figure the quickest way to find out is to help these fellers on their way and then Mike will be free to tell me.

"I notice our heros of last night are big-eyed and walkin' mighty careful, kinda like they're afraid of makin' too much noise. Every time Mike breaks out with a song, they throw him dirty looks.

"First off, me and Mike loads the corpse up into the buggy. It is easy to handle 'cause not only has rigor mortis set in, but he's froze solid as a rock. After that, it seems like I notice that our guests seem to relax somewhat and even help hitch the horse. But I notice them two feller's eyes are kinda buggin' when they climb in the buggy, and wavin' adios, they pull out for Flagstaff.

"Next thing I know, Mike is down on the ground in laughter, rollin' and holdin' his belly. I think maybe he's gone plumb locoed on me but finally he starts to come around and between fits of laughter he tells me what happened.

"'When I first see their layout yesterday evenin', I couldn't figure out what they had rolled up in that canvas,' Mike roars out, 'but they was kind enough to volunteer what it was! Well, I reckon that whiskey might have had something to do with it, but, anyway, when I seen you couldn't talk them into stayin', an idear comes to my head! I comes out to the barn and unrolling that corpse, I drag him around out of sight, then I rolls myself up in the tarp and just settles down to wait for our friends!' Between a half-wheez and a half-laugh, Mike blurts out the rest. 'They decides to load me up before hitchin' their horse. Bendin' down with one on each side, they are about to pick me up, when one of 'em says, "We better have a little drink first, huh?" I hear one take a drink and just as they are passin' the bottle over the top of me, I jobs my hand out of the tarp and grabbing the bottle I says, "Don't mind if I do, it's sure cold out here!" 'I'm sure glad they had left the barn door open, 'cause otherwise they would have tore it off!' Mike gasps.

"Guess that the corpse made the long cold winter worth while for ol' Mike," says Pat, "cuz up until that time, he had been purty hard to get along with, but from that day on, he sings and whistles till the spring brandin' starts."

Tip Takes
the Cure

There's always been certain occupations that was known for their hard drinkers. Some thinks this is on account of the lower mentality of these men that do these jobs, since they're mostly men that use their muscle instead of pushin' a pencil or manipulatin' some poor widow's mortgage. Cowboyin' is one of these jobs that I'm talkin' about. It ain't 'cause they got a lower mentality that they do these jobs; it may be they left the so-called civilized world just so they could save their mentality. After all, there's many a man that makes his livin' in the city and just as soon as this clock-watcher hears that five o'clock bell on Friday, he pulls out to the country to spend his weekend. There ain't nothin' in the world brings a man closer to the Almighty Creator and peace of mind than to spend some time in the middle of his masterpiece of creation. Chances are good though, that when this ol' boy unloads his campin' gear, he's got a case of beer iced down and maybe a quart or two of scotch. I don't blame this ol' boy for wantin' to get out of that smog and hurry-up and step-on-your-neighbor style of livin' of the big city. What I can't figure out is why this ol' boy brings his beer, scotch, and high falutin' mixes out to the country to hide from the rest of the world (or maybe his wife) to get drunk. No sir, I don't think them city folks have got any reason to look down their nose at these other fellers 'cause they make their livin' with their back; at least when they do their drinkin', they do it where the whole world can see 'em and they ain't so ashamed that they have to hide to get the job done. One thing for sure, most of these ol' boys from the so-called hard-drinkin' occupations don't mess up the countryside with beer cans and bottles. This open country is their home and they respect it.

There's two things that these hard-drinkin' occupations got in common. These men make their livin' out-of-doors with ol' Mother Nature as their master, and all are lonely jobs. Different from other men, these men don't drink to drown their sorrow but to vent their joy. When a cowpuncher goes to town, chances are good it's been anywhere from one to three months since he's last seen the bright lights. He's happy to be alive and he ain't afraid to let the whole world know it.

He's got all his wages in his pocket, barrin' what he spends on a new pair of Levis and maybe a new saddle blanket. The ranch furnishes all his groceries, so after he buys the personal things he needs and what he needs to keep his cowboy outfit in good shape, this puncher is free to spend the rest on paintin' the town! Some people call him wild, but this is just his way of tellin' the world he's feelin' good. It can get mighty lonesome stayin' in a camp by hisself, so, knowin' that he only has so much time and money to spend before he goes back, he tries to cram as much fun and excitement as possible into this short visit. No matter how long he spends in town, it's always too soon when the money runs out and it's time to go back to the ranch.

There's exceptions, but most cowpunchers save their drinkin' for town and most cow outfits frown on any drinkin' at the ranch.

Now I ain't sayin' that some of these ol' boys don't get carried away sometimes. I'm not sayin' that just 'cause they can't get to town every night, that it gives them a license to do as they please when they hit town. But, what I am sayin' is that town people don't understand cowpunchers. They don't mean any harm to anybody when they tip their heads back and squall like a panther, and if they happen to end up in a scrap with someone, they don't mean to seem wild—why, this life is plumb gentle as compared with the dangers and chances of any ol' "everyday" at work.

Like sayin', there's some who can't handle this fun-lovin' style of drinkin', and by the time they reach forty, they're pretty well hooked on the juice. It ain't hard to spot these fellers 'cause they're the ones that start buyin' whiskey so fast that it looks like they're afraid that the bar is gonna run dry before they get their fill! There ain't no fun left in it for them; it's strictly business. Sometimes it's necessary to haul these "ol' juicers" out of town and sober them up before they kill themselves.

Pat Cain knows one of these kind several years back. "Me and Tip was in Prescott on a blowout one time," says Pat. "After a week of this runnin' drunk and I see I'm not able to get any solids down Tip's gullet, I decide to load him up and head back to the ranch. Now he ain't real pleased about the thought of leavin' all this fine hospitality, but bein' he's drunker than I am, we go anyway. I take a bottle with us to nurse ol' Tip back to health with and there never was no doggie calf that ever liked his bottle better than Tip liked his. Fact is, he liked it so well I figured it best for me to keep it and give it to him in small doses—just enough to keep his heart beatin'!

"Well, I always believed the best way to get over a drunk was to sweat it out, and it didn't look like the Arizona sun was gonna let us down. Early the next morning Tip and I saddled up and pulled out. By nine o'clock the summer sun was bearing down and the air was so still we could hardly breath. Tip starts beggin' for a pull on his bottle and by one o'clock he asks me, 'By Gawd, Pat, what're you tryin' to do, kill me? I'm so sick I think I'm gonna die and I'm well enough I'm afraid I won't! I got the shakes and I'm pukin' every few minutes, won't you pleeease give me a drink?'

"Tip was sick alright but not near as sick as he thought. My horse had started lookin' back over his shoulder and showin' the whites of his eyes and his ears was a goin' a mile a minute. Glancing back, I see a mountain lion has fell in behind Tip on the trail! This lion is either old or sick, but either way, he's poor as a snake and I'm sure he don't quite savvy what he's doin'. There's many a cowpuncher that goes a lifetime, workin' day in and day out in lion country, and never does see a lion except maybe in a trap or one treed by some hounds. So when Tip spies this lion comin' up the trail behind him, it ain't no wonder that he gets a little worried. He knows he's sick and he's heard of fellers imaginin' everything from snakes to elephants.

"This lion has got him boogered, alright, but he just ain't sure whether it is real or not. Tip's voice was mighty weak and puney when he asks me, 'Pat do you see what I see?'

"Turnin' around and tryin' not to look at the lion I says, 'See what, Tip?'

"By this time, it looks like someone has whitewashed Tip's face and terror grips his eyeballs. 'That lion back there?' he barely squeeks out.

"Lookin' back over my shoulder again I scan the country behind us and with as straight a face as I can make, I says, 'I don't see a thing, Tip.' Then, kinda shakin' my head, I turn back around like I don't wanna believe what I'm hearin'.

"There was a long quiet spell, then all at once Tip shouts, 'Damn you Pat, you're goin' straight to hell! You do too see that lion! Oh, tell me, pleeease tell me, you see that lion!'

"I just kinda shook my head in disbelief and says, 'Tip, I've heard of fellers gettin' a case of the snakes before, but I'll be damned if I ever heard of anyone gettin' a case of the lions!'

"Tip starts sobering up right then and there and it looks like he's took the cure, for he don't ask for no more whiskey, in fact, he swears he'll never take another drink. He holds true to his word and don't drink no more. Well . . . , least ways not until the next time he goes to town, anyway."

COWMAN'S TROUBLES

Smokey Bear
and the BLM

▼▼▼▼▼▼

When ol' Brushy hears I'm puttin' together this book, he ain't long in gettin' to my doorstep. Says he, "I ain't a tellin' ya what to put in your book, but if you miss the chance to tell the great American public about the wonderful service the BLM and U.S. Forest Service is providin', I'll never forgive ya!" He says all this before the dust even settles. He's excited and I see I'm about to get another lecture from the ol' philosopher himself. I invites him in, and while I'm buildin' a pot of coffee, he keeps mumblin' somethin' about it bein' high time someone sets the record straight — let 'em have it, those scissorbills, four-eyed college boys, gunsels, and a few other choice descriptions that I'd quote but I know the editor would just scratch 'em out anyhow.

I finally gets my chance, when he stops long enough to lick the paper on his cigarette he's been buildin'. "Well Brushy, I sure agree with you, but this book is supposed to be on the humorous side and I don't see a damn thing funny about the forest service or the BLM!"

"You don't? I'll tell you what, you're too serious about life. Why, some of them government boys is the greatest comedians there ever was. Some of 'em has got kind of a twisted sense of humor, alright, but you got to admit that the whole setup ain't nothin' but a joke!

"Them boys has used a lot of propaganda to spread their idears amongst them city folks (they believe anything). I ain't got nothin' against them city folks, mind ya; they don't know no better. Them poor kids in town is raised up believin' these brogan-shod, khaki-shirted, tree herders is heroes. If you don't believe it, just watch a forest service truck drive down a city street sometime. I seen some kids snap to attention slappin' their hand over their heart like they was watchin' Ol' Glory herself go by! One kid even saluted! 'Course he was wearin' a Junior Ranger belt buckle he got by sendin' off a cereal boxtop. It makes your ol' heart skip a beat or two to see such patriotism amongst these youngsters! Now if you don't think that is funny, just ask some ranch kids what they think about forest rangers. Chances are good the answer might be somethin' like 'I'd tell ya, Mister, but, if Ma heard me, she'd whip me for sayin' them words!' Now, these kids ain't old enough to understand all they hear and it's a cinch they'd just be repeatin' what they overhear their Dad say.

"These hatchet-swingin' marvels of the forest go to college to gain all this humor they spring on the poor rancher. They learn how to play games, too. One of the games they learn is Hide and Seek. The rules to this game go somethin' like this:

1) All salt shall be placed from one-quarter to one-half mile from water;

2) All salt shall be placed off main trails and out of sight;

3) All salt shall be moved every thirty days.

"Now that's the basic rules and any rancher can play the game, even if they ain't on the forest. For a complete set of rules consult the forest ranger's handbook. The object of the game is to see how many cows can find the salt ground before it is time to move the salt! 'Course cowpunchers cheat sometimes by pushin' the cows off water and showin' 'em where the salt is hid. Most cowpunchers are honest, though, and bein' they got so many waters and cows to look after, they find it's easier to play the game straight. Makes 'em feel good, too, just bein' able to show them rangers how smart their cows is. The real humor is in watchin' ol' Bessie trail out to the salt ground she found ten days ago and find out there ain't no salt there no more! 'Course she gets a good chuckle outta this and rims right out with her nose on the ground like an ol' hound dog tryin' to find the latest salt drop. Naturally, the distance the salt is from water depends on the local forest ranger's sense of humor.

"Some of these rangers get to be such practical jokers that there's been a rancher or two that's got aggravated at 'em from time to time. Most of these ranchers is a surly bunch, though, and just don't appreciate a good joke. I worked for one of these sour-faced ranchers one time," says Brushy. "We're gatherin' a forest allotment and sure busy. We're gonna go onto the allotment with three different bunches on three different days. The boss notifies the ranger of the dates, 'cause he always plays by the rules. The ranger says, 'I'm sure busy right now, so I won't be able to make it all three days, but I will come out and count the last bunch through the gate.' Now this tickles the boss plumb to death. He goes along with the joke alright; he thinks it's sure funny that the ol' boy will trust him with his count the first two bunches, but thinks he better be there on the last bunch. He tells the forest ranger what gate we're goin' out of and what time to be there. We've been havin' lots of hot days and bein' that we got to trail these cows a long way before we can drop 'em, the boss don't waste any time. Now, the ranger sees this setup as a good opportunity to spread some cheer over this layout and shows up two hours late. When he sees that he's struck everybody's funny bone, he pulls his pickup right up next to the gate and mounts the hood to count the cattle. He's got his trusty counter in his hand and with his feet danglin' in the gate, he waves us to bring on the cows! Now some ol' milk cow might have took the gate, if her calf was a bawlin' on the other side, but I guess these cows don't like forest rangers 'cause they ain't about to go through it with him a sittin' there. The boss is all smiles ridin' up to the ranger and urges him to back up his truck. The ranger obliges and we put the cows through. The boss counts and so does the ranger. After they go through, the boss rides up to the ranger and asks him what he counted. The ranger's still full of fun and says, 'I got messed up. What did you get?'

"A man can forgive these fellers for what they don't know about cows," ol' Brushy goes on. "Trees, that's what they're supposed to savvy. So why's most of our forests nothin' but jack pine thickets, after a half-century of their management. I'm sure glad they got all that education to back up their management. I'm afraid to think what our forests would look like if it hadn't been for all that college learnin'. Now, I never knew about the Indians havin' any institutions of higher learnin', but I gather that they turned the forests over to us in better shape than what they are now!

"Wildfire! Now there's somethin' them guardians of public lands sure savvy and they always find it an easy way to get one over on the rancher. When a fire strikes these jack pine thickets, it sure wipes 'em out. Them rangers like to put on an act about how terrible it is, but inside they're grinnin' from ear to ear. When this fire comes along, it wipes out some of the sorriest vegetation man ever saw. The cowman hadn't counted on this piece of country for feed for the past twenty-five years, but now that the fire has come through, the grass grows and it's the best feed on the allotment.

"Mr. Ranger didn't forget his education and lookin' in his joke book he comes up with a plan that's bound to get a few laughs. First off, he tells the rancher, 'You're going to have to fence off the burn because your cows are going to trample all the fragile seedlings we've got planted!' The rancher thinks it's sure amusing that he's got to put out several thousand dollars to fence himself off the best feed his cows has seen in years, but just 'cause he's so hardheaded, he frowns. This gets to be a vicious circle and the ranger don't think the rancher has caught the punch line, so just to show he's still not out of jokes, he cuts the permit a couple of hundred head!

"I don't want it to seem like none of these ranchers and cowpunchers ain't got a sense of humor. Some of 'em is downright funny,

but they just lack the twisted wit that these educated men has got. I witnessed a time, though, when the ranger had to bear down to smile. It all took place on the Old Bar Cross Outfit. Dick ran the outfit, and although cookin' ain't his stronghold, he prided himself in his specialty: S O B stew.

"We'd butchered the evenin' before and Dick had tenderly nursed his stew all day like a mother would look after a sick baby. About the time he's ready to holler chuck, up drives a forest service pickup. Dick steps to the door and smilin' big and friendly like he hollers, 'Howdy! Better come on in and have some supper. We're just fixin' to sit down and eat a forest ranger!' "

Cuttin' Expenses

▼▲▼▲▼▲▼

Everything's closin' in on the cowman," says Brushy, "includin' the banks. It's a tough squeeze, especially for the small rancher, with the cost of everythin' goin' up everyday. Everything's goin' up in price except what the rancher has to sell: live beef! It has its ups and downs, but talk to any rancher and he'll tell you that the increase in the cow market just hasn't kept up with the increase in operating expenses. Now, the housewife will tell you that the cost of beef is plenty high, and as a result, instead of a beefeatin' country, the good ol' U.S.A. is turnin' into a country of vegetarians. Most of the country is becomin' addicted to soy beans and all the fine products made from 'em. Some people will tell ya what a fine meal they can make out of soy beans, but somehow I can't get real excited about sittin' down to a mess of soy burgers.

"I hear about one family that's havin' a hard time makin' it. They got five kids and the poor little lady has to figure out how to cut expenses. One way she does this is by cuttin' the grocery bill. She does right fine goin' down them aisles in the supermarket, just a hummin' and a tossin' the ready-made goods into her basket, but when she runs into the butcher's counter, she dang near tips that shoppin' cart over gettin' turned around. Beef gets to be a dirty word in this household and the kids get some age on 'em before they find out what cows is for. They get plenty of baloney and hamburger, but this

couple is so secretive that these kids got to ask their teacher what *steak* means when they run onto it in one of their school books.

"The rancher catches it from all sides, and it ain't long before he's tryin' to cut expenses, too. The cost of gas is puttin' some of these pickup-ridin' cowboys back on a horse. It's sure surprisin' to some of these ol' boys, that's got spoilt through the years, to find out that horses ain't so old fashioned anymore. 'Course the cost of feed has went up, along with grazin' fees, interest rates, vaccines, fencin' and other improvements, taxes, machinery and equipment, not to mention what kind of pressure the urban cowboy has put on the market to where a cowpuncher can't hardly afford to dress hisself.

"Every rancher has got his own methods of cuttin' these expenses but I hear tell of a new method not long ago. Bevin Clayton-Green, a native of New Zealand, come to the States to punch cows and see what he could pick up about ranchin' over here, and while he's here, he tells me about this new method. It seems there's an ol' boy over in New Zealand that's got a small ranch (they call 'em stations) and he's feelin' the price squeeze, too. Well, the place is fallin' down around him and he's got to have some fence built. So, goin' into town he locates him a fence builder and puts him on the job. He hands this laborer a few vague ideas about how he wants this fence built, givin' him the idear he ain't very particular, then leaves him alone for a couple a days. When he comes back to check on the progress, he throws a sure enough walled-eyed fit. He falls off his horse and lights right into this fence builder about his fencin' abilities, and he ain't a bit bashful about the words and names he uses to describe this fence builder. Now, Mr. Fence Builder ain't exactly timid and this kind of abuse he ain't fond of. Throwin' down his pliers, he takes to Mr. Rancher and thumps him quite soundly! When the scrap is over, Mr. Rancher is sure quieted down some, but if that fence builder could have seen the grin on Mr. Rancher's face as he jogged away, he'd a been bloody well puzzled.

"So far, everything is going to plan, and givin' the fence builder a few more days, Mr. Rancher thinks it's time to make another visit. Ridin' straight up to the fence builder, he begins by makin' some sort of apology, sayin', 'I'm a reasonable sort of ol' chap and I suppose you're an honorable sort of joker, so I'm willin' to let bygones be bygones. I'd like to apologize for the nasty tone I imposed upon you the other day and would like to seal it with a handshake.' The fence builder don't see nothin' wrong with this and gladly shakes his hand. 'Now,' says the rancher, raisin' his voice, 'I still haven't changed my opinion about this fence, though, and bein' I'm a sportin' man, I'll wager you that you can't whip me again. Mind you, ol' chap, there's no hard feelings, but a good scrap now and then keeps a man in shape, don't you think? If you whip me again, I'll pay you double for this fence; but if I get the best of you, you do the job for free!' The fence builder jumps on this offer like a dog on a bone and can hardly wait for the ol' boy to tether his horse. But, this time, Mr. Rancher has full control and he ain't slow in thrashin' the fence builder till he hollers uncle! The fence builder knows he's been set up, but it's too late to complain now, and besides, with this rancher a settin' astraddle of him, he don't think it would do much good anyhow!"

Horsetracks Keep
Men Honest

▀▖▜▖▜▖▜▖▜▖▜▘

F ences has sure changed the cow business from what it was years ago," says ol' Brushy. "There was a time when a cow could drift from the Mississippi to the Pacific Ocean or from Canada plumb into Old Mexico. 'Course that's stretchin' it a mite, but there wasn't no fences back then and many a cow brute has showed up in a roundup many miles from her home range.

"Back in them days, ranchers would get together every few years and decide to pull off a big general roundup, every outfit in the country throwin' together to form a pool wagon. This allowed the ranchers to straighten out the cattle and get their cows back home. Naturally, this had to be done every few years.

"It was only a matter of time, and sure enough, along came bob wire and fences. Fencin' the country was accepted by ranchers accordin' to their needs. Some liked 'em 'cause they claimed good water and range land and they wanted it to themselves. 'Course, if you was on the other side of the fence and had more cows than range land, fences was somethin' you wasn't too crazy about! Most of the big range wars that a man reads about or sees in the movies was started over fences. That's fiction. Most ranchers seen fences as a way to hold onto country and water that was rightfully theirs, a way of knowin' where their cows was and bein' able to keep 'em classed up the way they wanted. It also gave 'em a way of bein' able to keep their calves branded up without risk of 'em reachin' weanin' age in the middle of another man's country before they got branded.

"Cowpunchers is different, though," says ol' Brushy. "I never seen no love lost between bob wire and cowpunchers. It was that way in the very start and it lasted down to modern days. Old time cowboys and cowboys of today may have had different reasons for hating fences but the fact remains: bob wire is somethin' they all dislike.

"The old-timers saw it as somethin' that cut down their range and changed their style of workin' and livin'. A change they didn't want to make. The cowpunchers of today have accepted fences as a way of life but he don't like 'em just the same. Just ask a cowpuncher to fix or build some fence. Some will just quit right then and there; those that don't quit ain't none too happy.

" 'Course the ambitious man that carries a long rope has never had any use for a fence. Fences make it hard for him to practice his trade. Back in the old days, many a man changed title from cowboy to cowman by how clever he was with a rope and runnin' iron. Few of 'em make it all the way to respected citizens 'cause once a man's cows start to havin' too many twins, the man's popularity amongst his neighbors seems to fall mighty rapid!

"Fences, good brand laws, and good brand inspectors has kept a lot of honest men honest, but lots of horse tracks do more than all the rest put together. If a man rides his country and keeps his calves branded there's little chance for his neighbors to work on him. I hear a story a while back that proves my point," says ol' Brushy. "It all took place in a rough desert country. Two fellers (Dick and Harry will do for names) run their cattle in common on this piece of country. The cattle is wild and most of the cow handlin' is done on the end of a rope. Neither of these fellers is, or ever was, wealthy and they run sure enough rawhide outfits. These two ol' boys is barely scrapin' by in good times, and when it don't rain and the cow market takes a dip, it looks like they're gonna have to turn everything they got back to the bank.

"They're good friends, but when the times get tough, it's plain there's a limit to the friendship. They work together when there's somethin' that needs to be done but the rest of the time they prowl the range alone. This episode takes place in early spring followin' a mighty tough, dry winter. They've hired two cowpunchers for a couple of weeks to help 'em brand their calves, and it's from one of these I hear the story.

"This ol' boy tells me that by the talk around camp, he gathers that Harry don't spend much time ahorseback except when he has to, but Dick stays ahorseback all the time.

"When they go to work, they try to hold up the cattle the best they can, but there's some that don't hold up so good. They catch some of these and some of these they spill. Harry's got Dick beat for bein' a cowman. He's one of them fellers that don't seem to ever forget a cow and he'd have been the man to be in the lead except for his mild and soft-spoken manner. It's not that a mild and soft-spoken man can't be a boss, but Dick is loud and overbearing and it's a cinch that he ain't about to be second to nobody! So, just because Harry is a good feller he listens to a lot of noise from Dick and takes a back seat.

"They jump a bunch of cows high up in the head of a rough canyon one day. This country looks like the devil himself put it together 'cause it seems the only thing that grows in this boulder pile is chollas! When they start off the side of that mountain, you can smell their feet burning as   they boil down through the rocks.

These cowboys don't know what it means to pull up when they jump a cow and they're pushin' on their bridle reins all the way. They finally get them held up in a big sandy wash at the bottom but spill some of 'em in a mesquite thicket on the way. They all back off, givin' the bunch as much air as they can hoping they'll settle down some. Most of 'em has got their tongues hung out and they're millin' and squirm-in'. Purty soon they start motherin' up. There's a long-eared bull calf in the bunch that don't mother up. Everything else is straight.

"Dick and Harry ease around till they're next to each other and talk over what they got. Naturally, Dick takes over and is doin' most of the talkin'. He tells Harry that out of the dozen cows they got held up, there's only two that belong to Harry and they're both dry. Harry agrees to this but when Dick says all the calves are his and should be branded that way, Harry balks. 'Now, Dick, I know that big slick, blanket-faced bull calf belongs to me!' says Harry. 'I seen both him and his mother day before yesterday, when we was workin' into that saddle right below Black Butte.'

" 'Naw,' says Dick, tryin' to run a bluff over Harry like he had so many times before, 'that calf belongs to that big, blue, high-horned cow of mine that runs up at Horse Shoe Springs!'

"This time Harry thinks he's backed up far enough and says, 'Damnit Dick, I know what I'm talkin' about. We had the cow you're talking about yesterday and she's as dry as a popcorn fart! This is the calf I seen the other day and he was follerin' one of my cows. I seen her today, too. She was with that little droop-horned cow that got away when we went through them mesquites! Now, damnit Dick, I'm tired of this bullshit! You gotta learn that there's a *difference* between your cows and mine!'

" 'That's right, there *is* a difference,' says Dick, knowin' that his bluff didn't work, but holdin' true to his nature, he ain't about to let Harry have the last word. Stickin' out his chin and leanin' out of the saddle he jabs a finger in Harry's chest and hollers some mighty fine advice for his friend, '*Now* there's a difference, but you just keep layin' around camp and someday they'll all belong to *me*!' "

ON MULES
AND MEN

Pleasure Mules

▼▼▼▼▼▼

I was thumbin' through one of the leadin' horse rags the other day when I spies an advertisement that sure enough stops me cold," drawls ol' Brushy. "There was this here picture of a blond beauty a sittin' on a big good-lookin' sorrel mule. Now, by all standards, this purty young thing was put together right enough to suit any man. It's a common truth amongst stockmen the world over that any animal can be picked apart and fault found somewhere. In other words, a man can top his cow herd and say, 'That's the best cow I ever saw,' but he can tell you a dozen things about ol' Suzie that he'd like to change. Same thing goes for horses. There's always somethin' a man would change about a horse, no matter how well he likes him. But there's nothin' about this flaxy-maned beauty that I can find fault with. I can't tell whether or not this picture's been tampered with, but everything I see tells me she's an eyeful. Conformation-wise I sure can't find no flaws and they got her in a getup that lets a man see as much of her conformation as possible!

"The mule ain't no slouch hisself! I study him for a minute and decide that by what I can tell by the picture he's probably the finest hard-tail I ever laid eyes on. But the thing that catches my attention next is the wordin' in big black print. It says, *Pleasure Mules—A New, Pleasant Experience!*

"Lookin' at the picture is a pleasure alright but somehow I just got to believe that either the mules these folks is raisin' is outta a lot gentler stock than I'm used to or else (and I think this is it) the charmin' smile on that cowgirl has got just as winning ways with mules as it does with cowpunchers! I ain't one to knock another's way of doin' things, 'specially if it works, but experience has told me that if that heifer is gonna make a full day of ridin' that mule she better put on somethin' to protect that purty suntan she's sportin'. A cowpuncher wears boots with high tops, long handles, Levi's, denim shirt (always long-sleeved), hat, chaps, and dependin' on the weather maybe he's wearin' a coat and gloves. That's a lot of paddin'. It don't leave nothin' but his face and hands that's got to deal directly with the elements; I've seen cowpunchers that's got enough coverin' on to start a Salvation Army store and still get so skinned up that they look like a fresh-peeled strawberry in a jam factory!

"With that fancy gal astraddle of that good-lookin' mule, they probably got more orders inside a month than they can raise in ten years, but they ain't gonna trip me up with fancy pictures of good-lookin' women and such. I'll hand 'em one thing, though, any amount of time I spend with a mule, whether it's a ridin', packin', or drivin', and I escape with my life, I figure it's like the advertisement says — a pleasure and a new and pleasant experience!

"Some men get along better with mules than others. Nick Perkins rode a mule many a mile and he still rode 'em long after most men his age would be ridin' a rockin' chair. He raised crossbred brahmer cattle in rough country and he could do anything he had to do on a mule.

"Whistle Mills was another one. He caught more wild cattle on a mule than most cowpunchers ever saw. Neither Nick nor Whistle was a blue-blooded mule man; no, they loved horses and rode good ones, too, but they had that somethin' that let them get a whole lot more out of a mule than the rest of us can. I'll never forget watchin' ol' Nick on a long-legged white mule workin' a herd. It was quite a site to see him amongst them high-horned brahmers, but if a man chuckled at first, it wouldn't be long before he changed his tune when he seen what Nick could do on that mule.

"Not all mule stories are that pleasant. I get tickled when I hear some waddie brag about how much he's packed mules and never got in a wreck. I figure it's like the ol' boy that says he's never been bucked off. Hell, he's just tellin' the world he's never been on many buckin' horses. If you've packed mules, you've been in some wrecks.

"Sometime back I was workin' for the Diamond Bar in New Mexico. It's north of Silver City in the Black Range. The west boundary is on the East Fork of the Gila River and the east boundary is the Continental Divide on top of the Black Range. It's a steep and haired-over country. There's only a few places a man can take a wagon; the rest is a straight pack outfit.

"The owners of the ranch are cow traders and find some cheap cows in southern Arizona that were droughted out and on the lift. They sent word to Ben Fancher, who's runnin' the outfit, and tell him the cows are on the way. They bought two hundred of these cows but there was some had to be drug off the trucks. One truck turned over on the way into the ranch, and some of the cows found that an experience of a lifetime. It was a sad lookin' layout when they unloaded at the Links Camp that December day and them that had to be trailed the last six miles over that rough country looked even worse. I reckon things would have appeared a little rosier if there had been more feed on the Diamond Bar, but it hadn't rained the summer before and feed was plenty scarce. Ben ain't happy about this Christmas present his generous bosses send him but they ain't impressed when he objects. Anyhow, this leaves Ben with a bunch of droughted-out desert cows in high mountain country in the middle of winter. Seems only thing goin' our way is that there's no snow on the ground and not too cold—for the time bein' anyway. Ben knows these cows can't stand much chousin' and decides to locate 'em down on the Gila. 'Least ways we won't run out of water,' allows Ben. 'We're gonna run out of feed everywhere before spring, but these cows need somethin' extra right now and at least we'll have 'em where we can pack feed to 'em.'

"Ben orders a truckload of protein blocks, and they arrive a couple of days later. I inherit the job of packin' feed to these cows. I've got four mules. Two of 'em are sure good and have packed a lot of salt. The other two are broncs. Bringin' a couple of mules from Black Canyon, Ben joins me for about four days and we attack that truckload of feed. The best way to break a mule to pack is to pack him and I reckon them bronc mules felt like their whole world caved in on 'em! Ben stayed long enough to allow me to get a headstart on them starved cows. From then on it was up to me. I packed six blocks (two hundred pounds) on each mule, four days a week. These

were long, slow trips over that rough country. On the days when I was packin' to the closer feed grounds, I'd unload my mules and turn them loose to go back to the Links on their own, while I prowled my country. Packin' to the farthest feed grounds was a dark to dark trip with me trompin' on their hocks all the way back to camp, makin' 'em trot all the way. I was feedin' oats free choice to them mules, and after about thirty days, they was as tough and stout as any mules I ever saw. The outfit furnished good pack saddles, and keepin' the mules shod good, I never had a sore-backed or crippled mule.

"By the time spring came, those broncs were fine pack mules but they didn't get that way by accident. No sir, they got that way by *many* accidents! I hadn't been packin' 'em more than a week when we had our first serious wreck. 'Course we'd hubbed many a tree and scattered many a protein block over the country, but it had been goin' pretty smooth all in all. It was durin' this wreck I learned the reason why the Good Lord put long ears on mules.

"About a quarter-mile from the river bottom, on one of the trails I used, the trail drops off sudden for about twenty feet. My horse and mules got to slide down this on their hocks, so before droppin' off, I stops and checks the hitches and tighten all the britchens. Gettin' back on Buck, a big, stout, gentle horse, we start on down the trail. We got another hundred yards before we drop off and I'm lookin' ahead when Buck gets a hell of a jerk, and hearin' a commotion, I know the ball has opened! I don't know what touched it off but Miss

Kitty (one of the broncs) has got a hind leg over the lead rope of
Brown, the gentle and last mule in the string. Brown has sat back
and is sittin' on his tail. Miss Kitty's squeelin' and kickin' as hard and
as fast as she can. 'Course all this has boogered the two front mules
and they're tryin' to leave the scene! A few more kicks and a little
slack from Brown and now Miss Kitty has got a half-hitch around
her right hind leg and then Brown sits back again. This time, when
everything comes tight, Miss Kitty really gets stretched out. I have
bailed off Buck and with my barlow in hand I aim to see if I can cut
my way out of this wreck. By the time I get to Miss Kitty, she's lifted
plumb off the ground, upside down, and what I mean she's stretched
out to what looks like fifteen feet long! The two lead mules are
draggin' and pullin' for all their worth. Ol' Buck ain't helpin'; he don't
get excited and leave, but just kinda stays with the lead mule, givin'
him all the slack they need to pull. Brown don't like nothin' he sees
and has got his brakes locked up, and in this malapai country, he's
got a lot of boulders to brace against. I think Miss Kitty's gonna be
pulled in two before I can get her loose. All kinds of bad thoughts
are runnin' through my mind as I cut Brown's lead rope. I know I
got a crippled mule, maybe two, a tore-up pack saddle, maybe three
or four, maybe no horse to ride outta here after I cut this drag off

the end! It don't take much effort to cut the half-inch nylon lead rope; it's drawed down to about three-eighths size! When I cuts the rope, them two lead mules leave like they're shot out of a cannon and rim fires ol' Buck. Now, like sayin', ol' Buck has been mighty patient about this whole mess but when these mules rim fire him, he takes this as an insult and decides its time to leave! They left there so fast Miss Kitty never touched the ground! Buck's in the lead and I know this wreck ain't over yet. Headed downhill, this one horse-, two mule-powered freight outfit can't go far before it self-destructs. I can barely keep my eyes open when Buck makes a U-turn and I see that it's turned into a game of crack-the-whip and Miss Kitty's the popper! She's still off the ground about two foot and swingin' wide when they make the turn. This time Miss Kitty's got the leverage and her swingin' weight off the side turns the last mule over and rolls him over about three times. This added drag slows things considerably and brings the whole wreck to a halt when this drag line wraps around the bottom of a cedar tree!

"It takes a good while to straighten out this wreck but this time I'm able to untangle 'em one at a time and anchor each onto a cedar tree as I go.

"Brown's plumb confused by this time and comes trottin' right up to see what he's missed out on. As a rule, he's hard to corner and catch in a corral but he's so confused right now that he lets me walk right up to him.

"It takes me the better part of two hours to patch this outfit back together and gather all the protein blocks. But the thing that surprises me the most is that I ain't got a crippled mule in the bunch! Brown lost some hair off his hocks and rump bein' skidded over the rocks, but Miss Kitty's plumb all right. I spent a lot of time goin' over the wreck in my mind and the best I can figure out is that the reason Miss Kitty ain't lost no hide is that she's in the air the whole time and the best I can figure out why she didn't get crippled while bein' stretched is that all that extra hide the good Lord put in them ears was pulled down and gave enough hide to be stretched out and not pulled in two!

Reputations

▗▖▗▖▗▖

Horses and mules got personalities just like men do. The horse or mule that one man hates will be another man's toppy. A good hand knows this and will trade off a horse he can't get along with before he ruins him by fightin' him. 'Course I ain't sayin' there ain't some four-legged critters that nobody can get along with. Ask any cowpuncher that's been around the outhouse more than once and he'll tell ya stories about horses and their long-eared cousins that's got reputations as long and bad as any of the two-legged outlaws and carpetbaggers that used to plunder the old West. Some of these ponies are so well known that a cowpuncher in Texas might be able to describe one of these outlaws in Montana to a tee, even though he's never seen the horse before.

Ranches, like horses, get reputations, too, and sometimes that reputation comes from the horses. If an outfit gets a reputation for buckin' horses, it's a cinch that you ain't gonna find many cowpunchers that's past their prime a knockin' at the front gate. Them that's not willin' to climb anything that's drug outta the remuda ain't got no business on an outfit like this and they know it. They'll hunt a place where they can unroll their bed and sleep in it, not just lay in it all night and worry about what's gonna happen in the mornin'! These fellers lose lots of weight from lack of groceries, 'cause a nervous belly don't hold much chuck. When a man reaches this time in his life, his idea about horseflesh changes. A cowpuncher that used to be damn particular about how a horse was put together ain't near so quick to condemn a horse on his looks. As one of 'em once said, "Gentle is sure a purty color!"

Gentle horses don't make bronc riders though, and no one knows this better than the cowpuncher who's cravin' bad horses. To hand one of these fellers a mount of gentle horse is to take all the joy outta life. I seen this happen one time. Tim's the cowpunchers name, and when he goes to work, the boss gives him a mighty fine mount. He's got good drive horses and good evenin' horses, too. With the mount he's got, he sure won't be afoot, whether he's workin' a herd or leadin' a drive, but Tim ain't happy. After goin' through his horses once, he starts watchin' the rest of the horses and begins to set up some horse trades. Tim ain't learned to appreciate good cow ponies yet and life is sure dull. He ain't been with the outfit two weeks and he's traded every one of his horses off for the sorriest, trashiest horses in the remuda. The horses he trades for have got a lot of heart and they do their best to please Tim. I reckon they suit him, 'cause Tim starts jokin' and laughin' again.

Most of these "bad" reps (whether horse, mule, or ranch) got a way of growin' in size and fierceness the more miles there is between the cowpuncher tellin' about some caballo and that caballo. Same goes for good horses, too. If ol' Dobbin' is a sure enough good cow pony in Yavapai County, then by the time he gets told about up on the Sweetwater, he could cut pairs all day long and never make a mistake (and that's with nobody on him either!).

I seen a mule with a rep one time, but for some reason it never seems to get off the outfit. He's a pack mule and been on the ranch for a number of years. The outfit buys him when he's a bronc and sends him to a camp where Bob is stayin'. Bob ain't his real name but from the talk he hands me one time I gather he's real popular in certain parts of the country; but growin' tired of bein' in such demand for bein' the guest of honor at those parties that folks is throwin' for him,he pulls out one moonlit night and turns his back on all this fame. (Some say those were necktie parties, but I don't believe it.) Anyhow, when Bob comes to this outfit, he lands a camp job. He don't go to town 'ceptin' when he has to and that ain't but about twice a year. He gets his shoppin' done in a hurry and beats it back to the ranch mighty pronto. This solitary style of livin' makes

a man purty lonesome and Bob ain't no exception. About the only
thing ol' Bob's got to talk to is Blue, his hound, and his horses and
mules. He makes pets outta all of 'em. So when Bob gets this bronc
mule, it's like gettin' a new friend. Bob's a cowpuncher, all right, and
he knows how to handle a bronc mule, so he don't hesitate to foul
this new pet real proper while he's breakin' him. But it's later on, while
saddlin' him to pack some salt, that he finds this weakness this mule's
got. Liftin' his tail to put the britchen on, ol' Bob scratches this mule
a couple of times under the tail. The mule kinda stamps his hind feet
and wrings his tail. Bob don't take this as a good sign and jumps back
fallin' over the top of Blue, who's laid down in the shade of the barn.
Blue leaves there believin' the barn's fell over on him and yelpin' every
jump!

Bob's layin' there on his southside and propped on his elbows just eyein' this mule. The mule ain't none too concerned, and Bob can't see as how he acts like a mule that's been insulted, so, gettin' up, he eases over agin' the mule and standin' as far to the front of that mule as he can, he slips a hand around behind and under the tail and begins to scratch. I don't have to tell a man that he's bein' cautious, but he ain't so certain about the little mule's intentions on that first go-round, so when Mr. Mule wrings his tail and stamps his hind feet this time, ol' Bob stays planted. Bob tells me later that his head and feet was sure havin' an argument along about this time, his feet tellin' him to go and his head tellin' him to stay. Anyhow, his head wins out and it ain't long till ol' Bob's got this weakness of this mule figured out. It's right then and there that this ol' loner and mule sign a peace treaty that lasts until some of Bob's old acquaintances move into the country and, suddenly tired of the same scenery day after day, Bob decides to drift.

By the time Bob pulls out, he's showed some of us fellers his trick mule, as he calls him, and so the mule gets his behind scratched purty regular. As the years go by, the little mule got used to seein' many a stranger come and go at the camp. Most of these men didn't stay much longer than a year or so before they'd pull out to see new country. Finally, the mule wasn't so particular about who scratched his behind; in fact, if the urge struck him, he might come a trottin' across the corral at a man, whirl around, wringin' his tail and squirmin' his rump, come a backin' right up brayin' the whole time!

Like I said, it seemed like the reputation of this little mule never seemed to leave the ranch, but even if some new waddie had heard of him, it was more than most of 'em could stand to see this mule come a backin' at 'em and it was always good for at least one or two high-heeled stampedes a year!

"Stutterin' Sam" got his name from a run-in with this friendly little mule one time. Sam was goin' through the works with the outfit and had somehow never heard about the mule. When the wagon picks up the camp man that's got this hard-tail, he's packin' his bed on the mule and drivin' him and the rest of his mount. The next mornin' we're catchin' horses and Sam and part of the crew is holdin' the ropes while the wagon boss is catchin' horses. The remuda starts to millin' and directly the little mule is on the outside agin' the ropes. Sam kinda backs up a step or two, when he sees Mr. Longears comin' around,

not bein' especially fond of mules anyway. But what pulls the plug
is when this friendly little critter stops after passin' Sam and starts
to backin' at him squirmin' and wringin' his tail! Now Sam always
prided hisself on his intelligence but this was one time he didn't stop
to think twice! He turned loose of them ropes like they was burnin'
his hands and, squealin' like a stuck hog, he threw dirt all over the
poor little ol' mule diggin' his way outta there. It'd been a good escape
'ceptin' fer he got so rattled that his feet couldn't keep up with his
brain and they got tangled after the first two panic-stricken strides!
Tryin' to get up and lookin' back over his shoulder all he can see is
these two hind feet still a comin'. By now he's a movin' like it's the
end of the world and every time he goes to get up he leaves part of
him in the way and he just keeps a tanglin' hisself up and a fallin' on
his face. Finally, he gets her all together (everything 'cept his head)
and sure makes a fine run out of 'er. By this time, the commotion
has got the whole crew watchin' and we're all wonderin' how far he's
gonna run before he gets his wits back about him. Curly's there and
bein' a gamblin' man he starts to make a wager or two with some
of the boys; but his fun is stopped when the horse wrangler (who's
ahorseback) gets around Sam and gets him turned.

There can't be a man left amongst the whole crew that can stand
'cause they're so weak from laughin'. By the time Sam makes it back
to us, we've quieted down some but we all break down again when
Sam squalls, "That sssson of aaaa bitch! Ssssombody outta kkkkill
that fffflop-eared jjjjackass before heee. . .aw sssshiiit!"

FIRST DAY
ON THE JOB

Custom of the Country

I've always claimed that a hand is a hand, no matter where you put him," claims ol' Brushy, "but every time a man changes country, he's apt to get a new lesson or two. Cowpunchers travel a lot, 'specially when they're young, and it's plain that a man that moves around from outfit to outfit and from state to state is gonna see more than the man that travels the same trails all his life. All ranches work different, and it ain't long till a good cowpuncher can fall in and work with any crew and work any man's cattle whether they be gentle or wild or fat or poor. Mind ya, I said *good* cowpunchers, not *all* cowpunchers are good. But no matter how natural a cowpuncher is, it's a cinch that the more he travels, the more he sees and the more he's got stored up in his think tank to draw from.

"When a man leaves his native range, though, he becomes a stranger and most strangers are viewed through suspicious eyes, until that stranger can prove his worth. Ya see, man is a funny critter. Seems like he's tamped full of pride tellin' him that he knows the best ways of doin' things and has the best equipment to do it with. So when a stranger pulls into camp, it generally ain't long till he's put to the test. Whenever I see some ol' boy put to the test I remember a little incident that takes place up in Nevada a number of years ago. The way I heerd the story, there was two young Arizona waddies travelin' together. As one feller said, 'They was just big ol' kids that's broke loose from their dear mother's clutches but too young to buy whiskey.'

"They was driftin' through the country draggin' a quirt and lookin' for a tough horse to ride. These kind got it stamped all over 'em, so when they hire out to the Circle A outfit, the boss don't ask 'em if they can ride or not but figures he'll just find out before they leave camp that mornin'! When he ropes their horses and leads them outta the cavey, the rollers in their noses was sure rattlin'. All the advice he hands 'em, 'I'd use a snaffle on 'em if I was you.' Turnin' away he starts to build another loop. Then as a second thought he adds, 'You boys uncock your horses in that round corral.' I don't guess anyone will ever know whether his conscience got to botherin' him or if he just didn't want to waste the time chasin' loose horses. Either way, it didn't matter, 'cause these two youngsters was the first saddled and without even untrackin' these big thoroughbreds, they step across 'em. Needless to say, these outlaws done their best to hold up the good name of the outfit, but so was these kids ridin' to uphold their pride. Them big ponies bucked and bawled right through the middle of the rest of the crew who were still saddlin' up! I ain't sayin' that those boys didn't have to bear down to ride 'em but when they went through the middle of the crew they both squawled as loud as they could and the hair was flyin' every jump!

"Them boys stay on through the works and they makes good hands, too," says ol' Brushy. "But I witnessed a setup one time, though, that proves the worth of a stranger and later on the boss says he learns a lesson from his own orneriness.

"This is a rough country outfit in Arizona. No part of it is without rocks and brush but some of it just seems to stand on end. There's a Texan comes to work, I'll call him Taps, and joins the wagon when we're workin' one of the toughest pieces of country. He's a good enough feller, alright, and one look at him and his outfit and we all know he ain't no stranger to livestock. He comes to the wagon late one afternoon and we all get a chance to auger with him around the bullshit fire that evenin'. He don't brag and he ain't loud but he ain't shy either. Naturally all the boys pump him about news from his part of the country. We all know some of the cowpunchers workin' there, and Taps wants news about some of the cowpunchers he knows that are workin' in Arizona. 'Course all this talk leads to stories about some of those waddies. This Texan likes to tell stories about 'them big outfits in Texas' and he gets to soundin' like a Victrola that's got its needle

stuck on the word *big*. We're all feelin' like a bunch of small-time farmers sittin' next to this big outfit cowboy. Directly, the wagon boss (I'll call him Mike) jumps up and spittin' out his chew growls, 'Well, if they took this piece of country and ironed 'er out as flat as some of them outfits you're jawin' about, it'd be bigger than the whole damn state of Texas!' With that he strides to his teepee, mutterin' to hisself all the way. Mike's speech don't upset Taps none and everyone grins.

"Best I can figure, Mike must have spent most of the night dreamin' how he's gonna bring this Texan down to size and bring him to appreciate our country, too! Early next mornin', while drinkin' coffee and waitin' for Cookie to holler chuck, I notices Mike and Charley (the jigger) squatted down on their hunkers away from the bunch talkin' real soft like. Purty quick they both 'hee-haw', and slappin' his knee, Mike gets up and, with the biggest smile I ever seen, pours hisself some more java.

"I knew somethin' was up but didn't savvy until we start the day's work. About one mile's trot away from the wagon, Mike pulls up and spillin' his pills, he sends half the crew with Charley and he takes half. Me and Taps is in Charley's bunch and after trottin' a ways further, Charley starts droppin' men off. When he drops Taps off, I heap savvy what ol' Mike's hole card is. Charley drops Taps off on one of the trashiest, roughest points a man ever saw — any rougher and a man couldn't get off this point at all and down into just as rough a canyon. The holdup is at a tank on the other side. The drive goes smooth for the rest of us and the only one late comin' in is Taps. But when he does come in, he's got a little bunch of cows in front of him!

"Taps don't offer no comment 'til that evenin' when we're around the bullshit fire again. He says, 'Ya know fellers, I don't think I ever seen such a rough piece of country as what I slid off of this mornin'! Me and Berry got rock-locked more than once. If Berry wasn't such a good rock horse, I guess we'd be up there yet! I figured he could make it off, all right, but I was afraid to push him. You know, fellers, it's plumb hell if'n you don't know the custom of the country!' We all got a good laugh outta that, but it was several days later when I learn the reason why Mike don't enjoy it any better than he does.

"Me and Mike is trottin' along when Mike slows down to a walk and serious like he says, 'That Texan is a good hand, ain't he?' When I nod agreement, he goes on, 'You know, it wasn't no accident he

got turned off in that little piece of hell the other day. Me and Charley had that all planned out.'

" 'I had that much figured,' says I.

" 'Well, I was sure pleased how it turned out,' says Mike. 'I reckon he learned to respect our country and our way of doin' things, but he coulda hit me with a sledge and it woulda been easier on me than when he says that part about not knowin' the custom of the country! Hell! Right then I seen that if the tables was turned on me and I had to ride one of them boggy rivers or had to buck them big snows like I hear some countries has got, I'd be as lost as an angel in hell. You know, if'n a man don't know the custom of the country he's about as helpless as a newborn kitten—'til he does some time in it.'

" 'Yer sure right, Mike,' says I. 'A man is at the mercy of the country 'til he gets to know 'er. I remember the time I'm workin' for a desert outfit south of Rock Springs. It was a camp job and when the boss leaves me at my new camp he warns me that the water gap on the Agua Fria needs to be checked mighty regular. I figure that lookin' at the gap is a good place to start, so early the next mornin' I pulls out for the river. Now, when I gets to the river, it just looks like a big dry sand wash that's about a hundred yards wide. Away out in the middle, I see a small silvery sip of water that runs along for about two hundred feet then disappears in the sand. Bein' both banks is thickets of salt cedars and tamarisk that's too thick to travel and the country on both sides is steep and rocky, that ol' sand bed looks like just the place for me to trot up to the fence.

" 'I'm ridin' a big glass-eyed, bald-faced sorrel named Dollar. He's kind of a tall, narrow horse with lots of leg under him. All mornin' he's been a free travelin' pony and I been thinkin' how I'm sure gonna enjoy prowlin' my country on him. Turnin' him up the river, I figure I'll just trot up this super freeway to the fence. Soon as I turn Dollar up the river he just kind of quits me. I can keep him trottin' but I gotta gig him along every step. Lookin' back on it, if that ol' pony coulda talked, he'd been cussin' me purty good fer not havin' any respect for this river. He's doin' the best he can to warn me but bein' a stranger, or as ol' Taps said, "not knowin' the custom of the country" I don't savvy this sign language and keep him pointed right up the middle. The sand is dry and kinda crusty so we ain't sinkin' in and I'm sure enjoyin' just trottin' along on the level. All at once ol' Dollar just freezes up and I see what it is that he's been tryin' to tell me. The sand is cavin' in kinda like a roof might with too heavy a weight on it. Big slabs of crusted sand are tiltin' in with me and Dollar in the middle! Dollar kinda squats and quivers then lunges ahead as hard as he can. He makes a couple of lunges but he's breakin' through the crust now. He's fightin' hard but the soup that he's wallerin' in wears him out and finally bogs him down. I step off and not knowin' if I'm goin' plumb out of sight or not, I can tell you this peaceful scene a minute ago has broke loose into a man-swallerin' hole. I'm wonderin' if anyone will ever find a trace of me, when I stop sinkin' about halfway between my knees and hips. Dollar's quit strugglin'. He's layin' there just wide-eyed and scairt but he ain't no scairter than me! I can waller around some and figure I'm safe if I can keep movin' but I'm afraid Dollar's gonna sink outta sight.

" 'Right now I'm in a full panic and I figure maybe I can save my saddle anyway. Feelin' my way through the soupy sand I starts to undo my cinches. I guess my head begins to clear a little then and I realize that maybe ol' Dollar is doomed, but if he is, it's gonna take him a good while to sink to the promised land. I begin to hollar and wave my hat but he just rolls that glass eye at me. He's kinda layed over on his off side now and it don't look good. Next comes a double of a nylon rope but about all I can get out of Dollar is a squeal and one feeble lunge. I ain't thinkin' real clear again and wallerin' around by his head, I get one foot free and begin to apply my Bleuchers about his head and ears. I don't reckon I woulda won any medals from the Humane Society the way I massaged ol' Dollar's head, but it worked! Dollar just took so much of that and he come alive. This time he never quit fightin' until he got to the bank.

" 'The custom of the country allows that a man watches where the cows cross. Where they cross, a man can cross. I learned a lesson all right, but I ain't sure that Dollar ever appreciated it. Seems like bein' he was the teacher, he came out on the tough end of the deal!' "

Tom Goes
to Trial

▼▼▼▼▼▼

I don't suppose there's many men anywhere what ain't nervous when they first go to work at a new job. A man gains some confidence over the years but chances are good that he still feels like everyone's watchin' him the first day on the job. Worse than that, though, is that chances are damn good that he's right! It always appears that if a man is gonna make a batter, he'll do it while everyone's watchin', or he'll do it in such a manner so's how everyone's bound to find out.

I hear tell of a growing button named Tom Green that takes a job hoodin' for a southern outfit. This outfit is feedin' their remuda oats both mornin' and evenin'. Part of this kid's job is to hang morales on the horses after the crew leaves in the mornin'. These ponies have been grained for some time and they come in by theirselves. The kid gets along fine and after the horses finish eatin', he jerks the morales and turns the remuda out the gate to the horse pasture. He don't mind doin' the dishes, choppin' wood, and other chores the cook hands him. He wants to punch cows but knows most kids start out this way, and if he can prove his worth, he might be wranglin' horses next works. Someday he'll be a cowpuncher, but right now he's content to dream about it. All's he can think about right now is to show the wagon boss how anxious he is to make a hand and he jumps in and sure goes to work! Like I said, he wants to please and nervous don't quite cover the way he feels. He's so nervous that first day that he'd make a pack rat in a snake's den look comfortable!

By evenin', though, he's cooled off some and he's pleased as punch with hisself. But unknown to this button, his whole world is about to come crashing down on him. The crew comes in and the remuda is waitin' outside the gate for their grain. "Tom, if you'll let the ponies in, we'll hang the morales," says the boss. The crew has filled the morales and are waitin' to hang 'em. Tom throws the gate open and steppin' back, the horses come stringin' through. The first horse that comes through the gate comes trottin' right in, nickerin' kinda soft like and slingin' his head. Low and behold, he's wearin' a morale from the mornin' feedin'!

"Cheeerist! You better get your act together, kid, if you're gonna work here!" says the boss.

Poor Tom's ego fell a mile right then and his pride was sure hurt. But later that evenin', after he finishes washin' the dishes, unknown to him, the worst is yet to come. He's still got his feelin's hurt bad and feels mighty ashamed but seein' all the cowpunchers around the fire outside the cook tent, he just can't resist goin' out there to listen to these riders of the range.

He ain't no more than got to the fire when one of the punchers says, "This court will come to order! Will the plaintiff please approach this here bench and state the charges against the defendant?"

With that, Sam jumps up and standin' in front of the self-appointed judge states, "Yer Honor, the defendant, Tom Green, is charged with purposefully and willingly passin' hisself off as a hood! The prosecution will prove that, in fact, this kid is so green that he's in danger of bein' eat by those poor ol' droughted-out cows."

"Those are sure enough serious charges," growls the judge. "Does the defendant have counsel?"

Two cowpunchers jump up and before Tom can blink, drag the kid up in front of the judge. With the fire light playin' on the face of the judge, it makes him look meaner than a rabid wolf. He don't talk, he growls, and when he glares at the kid, a snarling grin peeks out from his haired-over face. He's got a gold tooth in front and when the fire light shines on it, it kinda puts Tom in a trance. Tom's knees are so weak they turn to mush and if it wasn't for the two cowboys on either elbow a proppin' him up, he'd melt to the turf.

"Well . . ., do ya have a lawyer?" snarls the judge.

Tom can't speak, he's so scairt right now he can't hardly breathe. He can barely hear the judge over the poundin' of his heart. When he tries to talk, his jaw is shakin' so bad that the words get chopped up and no one can understand him. He tries again but his throat kinda closes up this time and all that comes out is a squeak!

"If'n this kid ain't got no lawyer, it's up to this court to appoint one," says the judge. Lookin' around, the judge spies just what he's lookin' for. Back in the shadows is a wetback that come a walkin' into camp about sundown. He's lookin' for work this side of the border and spottin' our smoke he slides into our camp kinda careful like. He can't speak English but the boss savvies what he wants and in the best Spanish he can muster up he tells him, "No gotee trabajo but grab yourself some comida over yonder. Mucho frijoles, we gotee mucho frijoles." The Mexican picks enough of this talk apart to savvy there ain't no work, and after the Cookie signs it's ok, he fills a plate with frijoles and starts to fill his paunch.

Spyin' this beaner sittin' down with his back agin' a wagon wheel, the judge's eyes sparkle and with a raspy voice and pointin' says, "The court hereby appoints ol' Pedro over yonder there to defend the said accused victim of this court!"

'Course the Mexican don't savvy the judges words, but when all heads turn his way, his eyes get bigger than two corn tortillas. He jumps, but he's too slow, 'cause two cowpunchers got him collared before he makes 'er outta the light of the fire. He don't put up no fight, he's too scairt fer that, but he's beggin' for all he's worth. Draggin' him up before the judge, one of the punchers says, "Pedro, here, has agreed to defend the kid and presents hisself to the court!"

"Fine, fine!" says the judge. "The prosecution can present its case."

The self-appointed prosecutor, Sam, approaches the fire again and opens his case. "Well, yer honor," says Sam, gracefully bowing to the judge, then pointin' an accusin' finger at Tom, "Tom, here, come to this outfit yesterday and claimed he wanted to work! The prosecution upholds that Tom's a damn liar, 'cause the first day on the job he fails to complete his simple chores that has been bestoyed upon him." Clearin' his throat real important-like, he goes on, "Ahem, Tom has been given the responsibility of moralin' the caballos in the mornin' and any simple fool knows this means that he's got to take 'em off again', too! I have nine witnesses that will testify that they witnessed in effect, and after the fact, ahem, that said defendant failed to remove one morale and turned said morale out to pasture still hung on said caballo! Furthermore, we charge that said defendant is doubly guilty of conspirin' to do the boss a bad turn, 'cause the said hoss with the said morale was none other than the boss's top cuttin' horse, ol' Ace! In light of the evidence presented, then, I propose to the court, yer Honor Sir, that the maximum sentence be applied to Tom, here, for pretendin' to be a hood in good standin' when in effect he ain't nothin' more'n a gunsel kid!" With that, Sam, steps back, amongst the loud cheers and whoopin' of the other punchers.

Takin' his coffee cup and bangin' it on a rock, the judge hollers, "Order in the court! Order in the court! One more outbreak like this and ya'll be sortin' beans and peelin' spuds fer ol' Cookie! Now, Pedro, ol' boy, yer client here has got hisself in quite a jam and I reckon yer gonna have to habla up quite a storm to get him turned loose! So, now why don't you just give 'er a whirl 'cause this here judge is gettin' plumb tuckered from all this jawin' and I'm anxious to get on with passin' judgement on this here victim."

The two punchers holdin' Pedro shoves him forward to the judge. Pedro don't savvy what's happenin' but is plumb convinced by this time that it's him that's on trial and he don't waste no time sinkin' to his knees and begins to beg for mercy. There ain't one of these ol' boys savvies more'n a word or two of Spanish, but the way Pedro is rattlin' it off, there ain't no chance of 'em understandin' nothin'. Ol' Pedro's long-winded but he finally runs down some and it gives Tom a chance. He's finally come to his senses and he reckons he better put a word in for hisself, 'cause he ain't got much faith in his lawyer.

"Aahh, Judge Sir, I . . .," starts Tom.

"Shut up, Button! This here greaser is defendin' ya and the more he talks the better I like it. Hell, I can't understand nothin' that he says but by the tone of his voice and the tears in his eyes, I'd say ya got a damn good friend, here. If'n I was you, I'd let him finish. Looks like he thinks plenty about ya and I sure think he's sincere about it. I'm willin' to pass by judgement on ya and hereby's notice of pendin' probation. Mind ya, ya ain't scott free, I'm just suspendin' the sentence of a thorough chappin' applied forcefully to yer backside while bein' stretched over the wagon tongue. Like I said, this here court is just suspendin' sentence; one mess-up and your going over the tongue! Do ya savvy?"

Tom's so relieved he just stutters, "Yessir, Judge, sir, I'll do my best sir!"

Then bangin' his cup on the rock, the judge says, "Court dismissed!" The cowboys all come up off their haunches and are clappin' and cheerin'. They slap ol' Pedro on the back and pump his hand till he thinks his arm's gonna fall off! He still don't know what's goin' on but he can tell he's some kind of hero and he sure takes advantage of it. He's got his arms throwed up over his head like a victory sign and yellin' and grinnin'; he's sure celebratin'! This Mexican ain't no dummy, though, and amongst the hoopla that's takin' place, he works his way out to the edge and when he sees he's in the clear, he makes his break! In a flash, that greaser is as gone as a goose in winter and is lost in the dark. If it had been light enough to see, there would have been a string of dust a mile long while this wetback makes his escape from this bunch of locoed gringos!

Years later Tom tells me that he eventually gets a chappin', in fact, several of 'em. But he says he'll be forever in debt to that little ol' wetback that saves him that first day on the job!

Brushy Does
His Laundry

I ain't never worked in a country with big rivers to swim, so all
these tales a man hears about swimmin' big herds and horses goin'
under and bein' swept downstream are plumb foreign to me," says
ol' Brushy. "Most countries I've worked in, water's mighty scarce.
Dirt tanks furnish most of the water, storin' up the runoff from summer rains. What wells there are, are plenty deep and springs are few
and far between. Bein' raised in a country like this, a man don't get
much experience at swimmin' horses, but I come damn close to
drownin' a horse one time and I ain't even ridin' him. What makes
matters worse, it's the first day on the job and the horse is a loaner
from the boss.

"I takes a job with the Bar Cross Outfit. They're gonna start
the works in about a week, but Dick (the feller runnin' the outfit)
tells me to come on out and if I don't mind doin' a little footwork,
he can keep me busy till the roundup starts. I'm all for that, 'cause
this town livin' has got me broke and even though this burg looked
good to me a month ago, I'm tired of bumpin' into somebody every
time I turn around. I'm needin' some clean air and some room to move
around in.

"Showin' up at the ranch in the evenin', I start work the next day.
This Bar Cross is a straight bachelors outfit. There ain't no frills
anywhere, showin' that no women folks never took up residence here.

Sand Flat is the name of this camp and it's the winter headquarters. The house is a two-room bat-and-board type shelter with a wood cook stove in one room and a wood heater in the other. Most of the bats have fell off the walls long ago, kinda givin' a feller a feelin' of campin' in the open, but the roof is tight and if the wind don't blow too hard, a man can stay dry when it's stormin'. There's an outhouse up the hill and a barn that kinda leans over but still stands. There ain't nothin' fancy here, and a man knows when he drives up that this is a cow outfit, nothin' more and nothin' less. This modern age of computers and college-educated range managers (that spend more time with their butt plopped down on a cushion seat than in a saddle) has seemed to pass this outfit by. The money this outfit put back into the ranch goes to useful things, not to fancy play pretties. It sure looks good to me and when I roll out my bed, I feels right at home.

"Dick tells me the next mornin' that I'm to help Ted roll up an old waterlot that he's gonna rebuild. This waterlot surrounds a tank that's just over the hill from Sand Flat. In order to get there in a pickup it's about an eight-mile trip over a trail someone once called a road. Dick tells me he'll loan me one of his horses, so's how me and Ted can just trot over there. Meantime he's gonna gather the remuda, and he'll cut me my mount. He calls this pony Copper, and I gather Dick's sure fond of him.

"Ted and I trot over the hill and go to work. Hobblin' my horse, I see Ted loop his reins over the branch of a cedar tree. Thinkin' that we're purty close to camp, our horses are still fresh, and we're gonna by mighty busy with our fencin', I follow suit and tie Copper to a big branch, too.

"We start out by cuttin' loose all the old stays and pullin' staples. Ted is a workin' booger and he's got me humpin' to keep up with him. Directly, we got the wires on one side of the waterlot loose and on the ground. Ted tells me to start freein' another side while he rolls up what we've got. The horses are tied and hobbled right alongside the fence we been workin' on, so when Ted starts to roll up his wire, he's headed right at 'em. He starts rollin' at a corner, at the top of a hill, and bein' he's rollin' all five wires at the same time, he's nearly got hisself covered up from the horses' view. I often wonder what a horse thinks he's seein' when he spooks at a bush or rock or somethin' like that but it'd sure be hard to guess what Copper thought was a comin' down the hill at him!

"The first either Ted or I know what's happenin', we hear a loud snort and a breakin' branch. Copper snaps this big limb off the tree; first scairt by the rollin' wire, then by the branch, Copper is a runnin' backwards. We both start but we're too slow. There's a rock bluff about eight foot high right behind Copper and at the foot of it is the tank! Copper don't see nothin' but that big ol' branch that's chasin' him. He whirls to leave but the weight of the limb on the bridle reins keeps his head pulled around and he's leapin' as far as he can with them hobbles on and tryin' to kick this horse-eatin' cedar tree all at the same time! And that's the way he goes over the edge. He makes a big splash when he goes in, and when he comes up, he's swimmin' for all he's worth. He don't head to shore but straight for the middle. He's doin' good but with the cedar tree tied to his reins he finally gives to the pull and starts swimmin' round and round. Maybe the hobbles don't bother him much but it's a cinch they ain't helpin' him neither. It looks bad for Copper 'cause he's startin' to weaken and each time he goes around he's ridin' a little lower in the water!

"There might have been a better way, but at the time I couldn't see it, so pullin' my boots and puttin' my knife in my mouth I dives off the bluff. I pull up on the outside of his circle and when he swims by I reaches out and cuts a bridle rein. I stay wide 'cause I've heard stories of cowboys gettin' drowned by horses climbin' on top of 'em. I cut the other rein on the next lap, and Copper straightens out and heads to shore.

"When he hits solid ground, he lunges a time or two then comes to a standstill. His sides are heavin' and he can barely catch his wind. Catchin' up to him, I take my rope from my saddle, and puttin' a loop around his neck, I cut my hobbles loose. Copper rests a long time before he's got strength enough to even shake hisself.

"When it's all over, Ted and I have a good laugh; but while it's takin' place, it sure looks like doomsday for Copper. I slip down to camp and change clothes, then go back and help Ted finish up.

"That evenin' I see Dick eyein' my wet clothes that are hung up around the stove and even though he don't ask nothin', I'm sure he's wonderin' what kind of cowpuncher this is that's gotta wash his clothes after just one day's work!"

BACHELORS

Old Ben Fancher

ears ago most cowpunchers was bachelors," says ol' Brushy. "I reckon that was 'cause women was a lot scarcer back then. 'Course there was other reasons, too, like roads and transportation. The cowboys I knowed didn't own a vehicle. They traveled long distances by bus or train, and once they hit the town they was headed for, they'd set up camp at the local tavern, puttin' out word they was lookin' fer work. The bartender generally knew what was goin' on around the country, which outfits was working or when they was gonna start, or they'd know if some puncher had left somewhere, leavin' a job open. These bartenders knowed more about the cow outfits than the men that run 'em. Course all their information came from cowboys that had been sippin' the smart juice, so sometimes it wasn't too accurate. Anyhow, it wouldn't be long 'til someone come to town huntin' cowpunchers and he'd haul 'em back out to the ranch and put 'em to work. Most of the time it was a long trip over mighty rough and rocky roads. These cowpunchers didn't go to town every Saturday night. They might stay at the ranch for a couple months or if they was with a wagon it might be three or four months before they got back to town. Like sayin', it just wasn't as easy to get back and forth to town in them days, so even if a cowpuncher did find some gal he was sweet on, chances was darn good she'd done forgot his name by the time he got back to town!

"Yes sir, it was the exception, not the rule when a cowpuncher got married back then," ol' Brushy goes on. "Another thing goin' agin' the cowpunchers is the fact that most women want some financial security when they step into double harness. Now, most cowboys are financially independent alright—yup, they're completely free and independent of any finances! Cowboys never did earn top wages, by town folks' standards, and the wages they do earn just has a way of slippin' away once they hit town. Business managers they're not!

"Just seems like the good Lord just intended for cowpunchers to die out from extinction the way he stacked the cards agin' him fer marryin'," says ol' Brushy as he takes another chew. "Ya, it's a miracle he's still around with everything agin' him that way. You know a man that's stuck out in some camp with only cows, horses, and maybe a dog or two to visit with don't have much of a chance to polish up on his romantic lines. Not that they ain't polite; why, some of the politest gentlemen I've ever seen was cowpunchers. No, politeness ain't what I'm talkin' about. What I'm talkin' about is the fact that these fellers don't know nothin' but cows and horses. Bein' he don't get a newspaper delivered to his front door, he don't know nothin' about politics or about last month's social gatherin'. And I'll tell you from firsthand experience that it's downright difficult to keep some young lady's attention when all you know what to talk about is ol' Jaybird that tried to kick your head off when you was shoein' him, or the dead calf you pulled out of a heifer last week! Somehow women just don't find these things romantic.

"Even if a man did find a woman that was willin' to marry him, chances of findin' a ranch that had a suitable house for him and his spouse was mighty slim," says ol' Brushy. "They just didn't have them kind of quarters on ranches back then.

"I've heard some of these modern ranchers say they like to work married men; they say they're more permanent and don't quit so easy. I reckon as how they're right, but I allow as how the best hands are the ones that moved around a lot sometime in their life. There's plenty a time to settle down, but when a cowpuncher's young he needs to work for every outfit he can get to. That way he can work anybody's cows anyway they want 'em worked. Some of these ol' boys just never do settle down, though, and these ol' bachelors was sure enough cowpunchers through and through. They had just one love in their life and that was punchin' cows.

"Old Ben Fancher was one of these kind," claims ol' Brushy. "He was a cowboy's cowboy. Livin' alone so many years gave him a different way a lookin' at things and he seen a lot of humor in the things he done. I guess it was 'cause there wasn't no one else around to see the things he done that he got to watchin' hisself and, like he says, he got many a chuckle.

"One time he tells me a story," say ol' Brushy, "that most men wouldn't tell on theirselves, but Ben ain't worried about people thinkin' he's crazy because, as he says, 'they know I'm crazy already or I wouldn't be punchin' cows!' Ben tells me he's in a pickup, alone, goin' into headquarters to pick up some groceries. Well, as he's drivin' along his ol' mind gets to wanderin' and he just kinda goes through the motions of keepin' this pickup headed in the right direction. When he gets to the horse pasture gate he stops, gets out, and throws back the gate. Climbin' back in, he drives 'er through, stops, gets out, and shuts the gate. Ben never does tell me what he's been daydreamin' about but whatever it was it must have been good, 'cause he's still in another world when he climbs in the passenger side. Now, Ben always smoked Bull Durham and he says he pulls his sack and builds hisself a smoke soon as he climbs inside. Well, he's done rolled his cigarette, lit it, and settles back in the seat before he realizes they ain't moving yet. Jerkin' his head up, Ben looks over to see why the 'dumb son of a bitch that's drivin' this rig ain't took off yet,

"Ben never was the mar- ryin' kind, but he leads me to believe that he might have got married one time but the woman he's after says he's got to put down some roots and that in- cluded buyin' a house for her to live in. Ben just don't have life figured like that, so they never marry.

"It's many years later and neither one of 'em has married. Ben has just bought hisself a new teepee and he puts it up in his brothers yard so's how he can waterproof it. Seein' it all stretched up there clean and white puts a sparkle in this ol' gent's eye. Makin' his way inside, he gives his old girlfriend a call and allows as how he's finally decided to settle down and if she'll just drive on over, he'll show her the new house he's just bought!

"Yes sir," says ol' Brushy, "Ben was a cowboy's kind of cowboy. He went north in the summer and south in the winter. Fact is, he gets a knickname up in the Nevada–California border country on account of this migratory way of livin'. I hear the story from a rancher I run into one time in California. After we visit a while he finds out I'm from Arizona. First thing he wants to know is if I know Old Ben Fancher. When I say yes, he tells me this story. 'Ben had worked for us several different times and we always noticed Ben seemed to have a way of predicting the weather. He never showed up in the spring until all our cold weather had passed, and we could always count on our first snow a couple days after he left in the fall. He only missed once that I know of. I admit it was an early snow and it caught us all by surprise. When I got up that morning there was about four inches of snow on the ground and it was still coming down hard. Ben had beat me to the corral that morning and he didn't hear me coming up. He was brushing the snow off the back of his horse and as he puts the saddle blanket on, he's talking to hisself and says, "Sir Benjamin, I believe it's time to move to a warmer climate." From that day on, Ben was always known in this part of the country as Sir Benjamin.'

"One time Ben gets a taste of some of the changes that's takin' holt of the cow industry but rather than gettin' mad he takes it with a grin. Ben was one of the best cowboys that ever lived but there's a bookkeeper in northern Arizona that wasn't so sure about that after gettin' a taste of Ben's humor. Ben wants to go to work for this outfit but with a change in managers comes a change in some of the hiring policies of this outfit. When Ben gets to town, he goes to the ranch office to see if this outfit is hiring. When the bookkeeper says they are, Ben figures he'll hitch a ride out to the ranch to ask the boss for work. But like sayin', the new ranch manager has put in a new system and he's had the secretary draw up some job application forms. This bookkeeper's anxious to try out this new system, and before Ben can get out the door, he asks him to fill it out. Ben ain't never been faced with a job application before. Closest thing he ever saw to it was when he went in the armed forces — and he never applied for that! He got his name wrote down alright, but from there on he had grief. He stumbled his way through it, though, until he got to the part where it asked what kind of job he was qualified for. Ben writes "stock disturber." He hands it over to the bookkeeper and waits. Ben tells me later that the bookkeeper just nods as he reads along 'til he gets to the "stock disturber" part; that's when he raises his eyebrows! No tellin' what this wizard of figures is thinkin' but I got an idea he thinks he'll save the outfit a whole lot of trouble by headin' this cowpuncher down the road. He peers over the top of his readin' glasses at old Ben a standin' there and asks him, 'Have you got a drinkin' problem Mr. Fancher?' This don't phase Ben in the least and he answers as honestly as any man could, 'Yes sir, I sure do. Seems like every time I start to get drunk, I run out of money!' "

Coley

Their ain't nothin' ol' Brushy likes better'n reminisin' and when he squats down by the bullshit fire and starts to starin' into the flames it ain't long till he's gonna tell about some day gone by or some cowpuncher that's left us for the hereafter.

I'm with the R O wagon one time and we're camped at Triangle N when I see ol' Brushy hunker down this way and I know we're fixin' to hear some history.

"No one knows better'n me that I ain't a religious man," ol' Brushy starts in. The flames kinda light up his face as he talks and the many wrinkles that line his face shows he's got the years to back up his thoughts. "But someone tells me one time that the Good Book says there's some good in everyone. I didn't used to believe that, but, as ol' Father Time is catching up with me, I'm beginnin' to see the truth in it. Few years back I hear of a puncher that quits the country and heads to town. Seems like he got religion and one of them fire and brimstone preachers gets aholt of him and tells him he needs to move to town to do the Lord's work. What he found, instead, was that he was plumb out of place livin' in town and it wasn't how many times he attended church that counted but what he felt in his heart. Anyway, it wasn't long before he is lookin' at the tail end of a cow again.

"The thing some of these preachers seems to forget is that when God created this ol' world he had to make all kinds of people to take care of it. Each man's got his place and when he finds it, he just naturally figures this is what he was meant to do.

"Hearin' an ol' coyote like me talk this way has probably got you a might confused and you think I've done flipped my lid; but if you'll bear with me I'll tell ya what brings on all this talk.

"Campin' here at Triangle N got me to thinkin' about ol' Coley Lyons. It's a strange fact but when someone leaves this ol' world it sure makes a man think. I got an idea   that's somethin' the good Lord built into man so's maybe   he'd kinda take a look at hisself now and again.

"I got a lot of respect for cowpunchers and when I'm camped in a country that a man lived and worked on as long as Coley did in this country I can't help but feel a mite humbled by it.

"Some of you fellers know I've went plumb crazy by now. I know what your thinkin', 'specially if you hadn't worked with Coley the last ten years of his life. He mellowed out a bunch those last few years but before that he was purty tough to get along with. He was one cranky old booger around a crew back then. Fer the life of me I couldn't figure why an outfit would even keep him around. But like I was sayin' about a man havin' his callin' in life, Coley's callin' was that of a loner. There wasn't nobody that was ever more content than ol' Coley was to live and work by hisself.

"Now I don't know as how Coley ever spent an hour in a church, but I can say he spent his life takin' care of God's creation and he done it honestly, too. He always earned his wages — a company man all the way through. He might not agree with what the company was havin' him do, but if they said do it, he did it. Your askin', how does religion come into this? Well, if a man is drawin' wages to do a job, and he don't do it or he don't do it the best way he can, then when he gets that check, he's done stole from the outfit!

"I don't think Coley ever stopped and thought about things that way, but from the way he talks in his later years, he tips his hand that it was just inside of him to do the best he could. From what he says I don't think he ever worried about cheatin' the company but I think he did worry about cheatin' the livestock he took care of. I don't care how wet, dry, hot, cold, windy, or how tired he might be; if he thought there was somethin' that needed his attention, you can bet he'd be taken care of it. Somehow I got to believe that a man that lives by hisself for so long and don't have a boss a lookin' over his shoulder all the time and never lets up has to be answerin' to a callin' of sorts.

"Coley lived by ol' Mother Nature's rules; he never fought her. And you know I think he come about as close to figurin' her out as anyone I ever knew. He saw a lot around him most men might miss. When you went by his camp he might tell you that the walnut trees up in Moffit Canyon sure have a lot of walnuts this year, or he might say there's sure a lot of baby quail, or maybe he'd say somethin' about how the weather just ain't actin' normal, or like one time he tells me that the deer still hadn't shed off their winter hair! Hell's fire, any man might notice these things, but Coley put a lot of importance on 'em! This country was his home and he knew what was goin' on in it.

"When it come time for ol' Coley to step down and let someone else take over his camp, he done it; he didn't wait for the boss to come around and tell him he couldn't handle it anymore. He knew better than anyone whether or not he was doin' the job. So Coley left his camp when he felt hisself beginnin' to slip, not after he'd slipped.

"Coley knew his time was comin' and he goes about gettin' his country in shape for some other cowpuncher to take it. He done a damn thorough job of it, too. I rode into Triangle N one day, and Coley meets me with a grin from ear to ear. 'Well', he says, 'finished a job today that I started a long time ago. You know that old fence down in the bottom of Cow Creek? I started to roll it up before World War II. I never got a chance to finish the job 'cause Uncle Sam sent me his greetings, but I finished 'er up today! Guess it wasn't all that important but I hate to leave somethin' undone for someone else to finish.' He done this in 1978, just before he moved to headquarters!

"Sometimes a man's outer crust don't show what the inside man is like. This held true with Coley. Tough as he was, he had a soft spot in him, too. Now, he'd been with the wagon a couple a weeks when one evenin' he says he's gonna trot back to Triangle N to look things over. That seemed natural enough but then he says, 'Like sayin, I wanna check on Fluffy (one of his cats). She's fixin' to have kittens.' As he pulls his cinches tight he looks back over his shoulder and says, as if to set the record straight, 'There ain't nothin' special about that cat, but, like sayin', she's mine!'

"Coley loved a good laugh, too, and he had a few favorite stories he told. The trouble with Coley's stories was that he seldom ever got the story told that he started out to tell. There'd be somebody or something in one story that would remind him of another. 'Like sayin',' he'd say (he started damn few sentences without—Like sayin' on the front of it), 'that was when Oscar Coleman was managin' the outfit. We were bringin' the cut out of Mahone. We had close to a hundred head of yearlin's and everything is goin' pretty smooth 'til we started off into Pine Canyon. Like sayin', when them yearlin's tipped off into the canyon, they just gained speed and by the time the leaders hit the bottom they splattered all to hell! John Brown was in the lead and was tryin' to get around them that went down the canyon. He got the leaders held up about a quarter of a mile down the canyon!'

"Up until now ol' Coley's story has been goin' good and you'd think he was gonna get through the story all in one piece, but, oh no, like sayin', about the time the yearlin's splattered, so did Coley's story!

" 'There was a young kid workin' here who was trompin' on John's heels goin' down the canyon. I don't believe John could have got 'em stopped by hisself as thick as the brush was, but with the kid's help they get 'em turned around.' Coley pauses thoughtful-like, then goes on. 'This is the kid John Brown hires the fall before. He brought him out to the ranch one evenin'. The next mornin' the crew is shoein' up for the fall works. Oscar drives up and walkin' into the corral he spies this young kid shoein' a horse. Soon as he gets a chance he comments to John about how he ain't runnin' no gol-danged nursery and asks if he thinks that kid's a mite young to be goin' with the wagon. Like sayin', John thinks for a minute then says real deliberate like, "he's young alright but he'll age to beat hell around here!"

" 'Like sayin', this kid's shoein' a horse that had been crippled by a feller a couple years before who goes to work for the outfit when we're camped at West Split. Charlie Greene brings him out to the wagon. He's from the plains country and he ain't never shod a horse before, 'course nobody here knows that and this feller's got too much pride to ask for help. Well, it's in the evenin' when he's got to shoe a horse. The rest of the crew is up at the wagon drinkin' coffee and waitin' for the cook to holler chuck. Directly this new hand gets finished, turns his horse loose and walks up to the wagon. As he pours hisself a cup of coffee he comments, "Boy, he was a dirty, foot jerkin' son of a gun!"

" 'When he says this, he's got everyone's attention 'cause, like sayin', the whole crew knows the horse is a pup to shoe. "I got him, though," he goes on. "Only one nail showed up and no one ought to notice it!"

" 'Like sayin', the country was in the best shape I'd ever seen it, before or since. Boy the yearlin's was sure big and fat. They was packin' so much tallow, they'd get hot goin' downhill. Like sayin', I seen a big steer melt down goin' from Wildhorse to Cabin Dam. He laid down under that big juniper above Long Canyon where the trail goes off. It was that tree that Tom necked that big steer to when he was workin' here in the '60s. He was ridin' ol' one-eyed Mike. Like sayin', he was sure a good horse and he only had one good eye. Blinder'n a bat in the other. You wouldn't think he'd be much good in a rough country but he was as good a horse as a man ever rode anywhere you put him. He was good in a herd, too. He'd keep his good eye on what it was you was tryin' to cut out. Like sayin', he was a chestnut sorrel but he didn't like a breast collar. Put a breast collar on him and he'd act like a cinchy horse. 'Course, like sayin', Tom was a good hand with a horse anyway. He could make a sorry horse look good. He could make a good horse out of a sorry one or a good mule out of a sorry one. Like sayin', when he took that Sandstone camp he had two mules to scatter salt. One of 'em was a good pack mule, the other was as sorry as they come. Like sayin', one day he's leavin' to pack salt over to Wilderman Tank. He's got his mules tied up and he's puttin' the pack saddles on. Like sayin', Whistle had just had a new riggin' put in one of these saddles. He didn't very often spend money on things like that but this one saddle had got to where it had more balin' wire on it than leather. The tree had been broke one time, too. It was held together with rawhide. Another cowpuncher did that patchin' job. Like sayin', he was mighty handy with rawhide. He liked to get the hide off an old poor cow that had died. He claimed it made better rawhide than that offen' a fat beef. Like sayin', he shoulda known 'cause he worked a lot in southern Arizona and even worked for a while in Old Mexico. . . .'

"Now how we got from the bottom of Pine Canyon to Old Mexico, I'll never know," says ol' Brushy. "I'm not sure even Coley knowed how he done it. But, then, like sayin', who cares?"